A Duet of One

THE ASHTAVAKRA GITA DIALOGUE

Translation and Commentary by

RAMESH S. BALSEKAR

Books by Ramesh S. Balsekar

- Pursue 'Happiness' And Get Enlightened (2008)
- Celebrate the Wit & Wisdom: Relax and Enjoy (2008)
- Pointers From Ramana Maharshi (2008)
- Koun Parvah Karto?! (Marathi 2008)
- Does The Human Being Have Free Will? (2007)
- Enlightened Living (2007)
- A Buddha's Babble (2006)
- A Personal Religion Of Your Own (2006)
- The Essence of The Ashtavakra Gita (2006)
- The Relationship Between 'I' And 'Me' (2006)
- Seeking Enlightenment – Why ? (2005)
- Nuggets of Wisdom (2005)
- The End of The Seeking (2005)
- Spiritual Search Step By Step (2004)
- Confusion No More (2003)
- Guru Pournima (2003)
- Advaita and the Buddha (2000)
- It So Happened That... The Unique Teaching of Ramesh S. Balsekar (2000)
- Sin and Guilt: Monstrosity of Mind (2000)
- Meaningful Trivialities from the Source (2000)
- The Infamous Ego (1999)
- Who Cares?! (1999)
- The Essence of the Bhagavad Gita (1999)
- Your Head in the Tiger's Mouth (1997)
- Consciousness Strikes (1996)
- Consciousness Writes (1996)
- Consciousness Speaks (1995)
- The Bhagavad Gita – A Selection (1995)
- Ripples (1994)

A Duet of One

THE ASHTAVAKRA GITA DIALOGUE

Translation and Commentary by
RAMESH S. BALSEKAR

Advaita Press

Copyright ©1989 by
Ramesh S. Balsekar

First Published in United States Of America by
ADVAITA PRESS
P.O. Box 3479
Redondo Beach, California 90277

Edited and Designed by: Wayne Liquorman
Cover Design: JohnMcClung
Cover Illustration: Don McClellan

Library of Congress Catalog Card Number 89-84929

ISBN 0-929448-11-1   0 9 8 7 6 5

Contents

❧

PREFACE

A clearly seen feature of Eastern scriptures is the recurring repetition of the basic Truth in its different aspects, detailed in different words and with different illustrations and examples. The intention is to give a reasonable chance to the disciple with the least intelligence.

In the *Ashtavakra Gita* also, a considerable amount of repetition is found. One specific advantage of such repetition is that for some mysterious reason, a certain statement will have a sudden impact on a particular person at a particular moment, even though that statement may have been repeated several times earlier. And even for those who have already understood something very clearly, a particular statement made in a particular context often brings out a subtle aspect which had earlier escaped their attention. It is therefore important not to take a repetition lightly as a mere repetition. It is important to remember that when the *guru* makes a statement, it comes out of his lips spontaneously at that *kshana* or split-second. For him it is not a repetition, and therefore it has a certain special significance in regard to a particular context or circumstance. It is important to listen to every statement of the *guru* as a fresh lesson, and not to ignore it as a mere repetition. Even good music is listened to over and over again, and great sensual pleasure is derived from such music. How much more important it must be to listen to the Truth from the *guru*'s lips over and over again even though it is the same Truth!

Indeed, life itself is a rotating repetition. Day in and day out, year in and year out, there is repetition: morning, noon, evening and night; summer, autumn, winter and spring. But each has its own aspects which are rarely similar in every respect to the earlier ones.

CHAPTER ONE

✣

There is an ancient treatise in Sanskrit—some scholars consider it older than the *Bhagavad Gita*—called *Ashtavakra Gita* which consists of a dialogue between the sage Ashtavakra and his disciple King Janaka. This dialogue provides an extraordinary instance of the divine element in the relationship between a Self-realized *guru* and a superbly "ripe" disciple, i.e. one who is just waiting for that one quick spark of initiation into Truth that brings about sudden enlightenment. The *Ashtavakra Gita* at the same time provides an astonishingly direct, positive and unequivocal exegesis of the doctrine of nonduality, perhaps the best that has ever been done.

The *Ashtavakra Gita* is not nearly so well known as the *Bhagavad Gita* for the very reason that it is so specifically clear and unambiguous that it does not lend itself to the twists and turns required by commentators to justify their own philosophical pre-possessions or spiritual leanings. It contains superbly authoritative statements and clear assertions, so obviously based on intuitive experience and conviction as to deny and utterly negate any effort at exegetic ingenuity or intellectual acrobatics. It is a comparatively small treatise, compact and well-knit, containing about 300 verses of two lines, conveying the Truth, the whole Truth, and nothing but the Truth.

The sage Ashtavakra was so called because he had eight curves or deformities in his body. There are differing accounts concerning the deformities. One legend has it that when Ashtavakra was in his mother's womb, his father used to recite the *Vedas* every day, and Ashtavakra used to hear them so recited. The father, though a devout and pious man, was not a very scholarly man and thus used to commit a number of mistakes in reciting the *Vedas*; and Ashtavakra, already highly mature spiritually, could not bear to hear the *Vedas* so badly recited with the result that he could not help squirming in his mother's womb and thereby becoming deformed in eight places.

There is another legend in the *Mahabharata* that Ashtavakra's father, Kahor used to recite the *Vedas* to his wife Sujata when their child was in Sujata's womb. The child, one day, suddenly cried out "Through your grace, my dear father, I have learnt all the *Vedas*, but it is a pity that you commit several mistakes in your pronunciation." Kahor, a great scholar (according to this version) and renowned for his learning, could not bear this insult from his unborn child, and cursed him that he would be born with eight curves in his body, and thus was born Ashtavakra, "eight-curved."

The story continues that Ashtavakra's father, Kahor, went to the court of King Janaka in order to obtain some favor, and was asked to debate on spiritual matters with the court scholar named Vandin who was the son of King Varuna. Kahor was defeated and as a result was banished to the netherworld as a priest at a sacrifice being performed by Varuna. When Ashtavakra was twelve years old, he heard of his father's plight and went to the court of King Janaka in order to participate in a general debate where the most renowned scholars were invited. Ashtavakra found it difficult to get entrance into the court, but finally managed to do so. When the assembly saw Ashtavakra waddling into the court, all the assembled scholars began to laugh, even the kindly and pious King Janaka could not suppress a smile, but his amusement turned into astonishment when he saw that young Ashtavakra was laughing as loudly as anyone else. The king turned to the little deformed character and said to him, "Young man, I can understand why the others are laughing, but I cannot understand the cause of your laughter." Ashtavakra suddenly became serious and told the king that he was laughing because he could not understand how the king could expect to find Truth in an assembly of cobblers. Now the king was angry, and gravely asked Ashtavakra to explain himself. The young lad answered equally gravely, "It is simple, your Majesty. All these honored guests are no better than cobblers because they cannot see beyond the skin. They cannot see the Presence within the physical body. If the earthen pot is broken, does the space within get broken? If the pot is misshapen, does the space within get misshapen? My body may be deformed but 'I' am infinite and limitless." The king, already highly advanced spiritually, knew at once that Ashtavakra was a completely Self-realized soul, and the very next day, at his request, he was accepted by Ashtavakra as a disciple.

This story of Ashtavakra, like others concerning many other saints and sages and prophets is obviously not to be taken literally. It is not difficult to see the real significance of this story, as in the case of similar stories concerning other sages and prophets like the Buddha and Lao Tzu and Zarathustra. In the case of Ashtavakra, the deformation of the body in eight places could have a reference to the eightfold path of Yoga. Ashtavakra avers that enlightenment does not really need any practices and disciplines of body or mind. Enlightenment can be sudden and can occur in a split-second as soon as there is clear realization (not a mere intellectual understanding) that there never has been any bondage for anyone, that one is always free, that freedom has always been one's birthright.

Thus, there is the legend that the Buddha was born on his feet, with his mother in the standing position; instead of falling, he took seven steps and at the eighth step, he halted and made his four basic pronouncements: *samsara* means unhappiness; it is possible to overcome unhappiness; there is a way to overcome unhappiness; the state of happiness is *nirvana*.

In the case of Zarathustra it is said that unlike any other new-born infant, he let out not a cry but a huge laugh because he considered that life was meant to be enjoyed (subject to not making others unhappy). "Good thoughts, good words, good deeds" was the essence of his teaching. His is the only religion in which fasting, in the normal course, is not only not recommended but specifically forbidden.

Lao Tzu was supposed to have been eighty years old when he was born. The obvious import of the legend being not that he was in the mother's womb for eighty years but that he was conceived in wisdom and was born wise, and lazy! His teaching, astonishingly similar to that of Nisargadatta Maharaj, did not involve any practices or disciplines. He held that there is no goal and no path, and that the deep and clear understanding of the perfection of What-Is does not need eighty years for fulfillment but, on the contrary, can bring about sudden and instant enlightenment.

It is for this reason that the many legends and myths in religions are obviously not to be taken literally. They are supposed to convey the significance of the particular teaching in a quick, graphic way; to convey that the seed contains the potential which cannot be seen in the seed. Indeed, those who have seen someone as the "seed", as an infant and a young man, find it difficult to accept him as a sage in later life. You will often hear it said, "Believe me, I have known him since he was a child, and there was nothing of the sage or the saint in him." For many years, Ramana Maharshi, the sage of Arunchala in Southern India, remained in a cave all by himself, and in the meanwhile his family had given up all search for him. Then, when his whereabouts became known, efforts were made to get him back home, but all to no avail. Ultimately, when his own mother went to him and asked him to return home with her, he was forced to tell her that he was no longer the man who had left home, that that man did not exist any longer.

The dialogue between Ashtavakra and Janaka begins with the question:

"How can knowledge be acquired? How can liberation be attained? How can renunciation come about?" (1)

The very first question of the disciple is intensely significant to the *guru*. It tells him the general level and conditioning of the disciple. It tells him at what point in the spiritual evolution the disciple is at that moment. What is it that the disciple is truly seeking? That is what interests the *guru* most because on that will depend the *guru*'s answers and advice. Nisargadatta Maharaj asked me, when I first met him, what I wanted from him. My answer was, "I am not interested in happiness and unhappiness in this world or any other world. What I want to know from you is that Truth, that unchangeable Truth which has always existed and will always exist, irrespective of any prophet or any religion." Maharaj looked at me intently for a while, then smiled and changed the subject. By that time, others had come into the room and the usual session was about to start.

A certain amount of confusion and misunderstanding comes about because an important point is not always borne in mind regarding the relevance of the *guru*'s answer. The *guru* is not really concerned with answering the disciple's question as such. The *guru* is truly concerned with the conditioning under which the disciple suffers, and the disciple's questions reveal this conditioning. The *guru* is primarily concerned with removing this conditioning. The disciple is initially concerned with "acquiring" knowledge at an intellectual level. The *guru* is fully aware that there is no such thing as ignorance which could be removed by the acquisition of knowledge. He knows that every individual is the universal Consciousness which has identified itself with the individual body-mind organism, and that such identification is itself the ignorance that the disciple talks about. The disciple thinks that it is the acquisition of knowledge which will get rid of the ignorance while the *guru* knows that ignorance is itself the result of the positive action of identification. Any further positive action on the part of the illusory individual, such as any practices or disciplines, would only make the identification stronger. The *guru* must therefore, proceed cautiously and yet boldly to guide the disciple in such a way that the disciple finds (or thinks he finds) the answers himself.

An astonishingly vibrant example of this phenomenon is seen in this dialogue between Ashtavakra, the *guru*, and his mature disciple, King Janaka. It was quite obvious from the fact that the king had arranged an assemblage of the wisest and the most learned scholars in the realm for a discussion on spiritual matters, that the king was not a novice in spiritual matters, though perhaps not a little confused by the diverse and opposing views and opinions on the subject. At the same time, Ashtavakra must have been impressed by the sincerity with which Janaka was seeking his guidance, the humility of his approach, and the quality of his basic question. Janaka was not concerned with being entertained by the forthcoming debates between the scholars. He was not interested in sin and merit, hell and heaven. He was deeply concerned with the question: how can liberation be attained? He was aware that there cannot be any liberation without dispassion, and so he further asks: how can dispassion come about?

Ashtavakra answers:

"My child, if you are seeking liberation, shun the objects of the senses like poison; and seek

forgiveness, sincerity, kindness, contentment and truth like you would seek nectar." (2)

It is necessary to give considerable attention to this direct and clear answer given by the *guru* to a direct and clear question of the disciple. To begin with, Ashtavakra could have dissected the disciple's question and cross-examined him on what he specifically meant by each word. Indeed such an approach would certainly be resorted to by the *guru* at a certain stage of their relationship, but in the very beginning it is necessary to establish the foundation of a healthy relationship. The *guru* starts with the words "My child." These two words are very significant in several ways. They tell the disciple in unequivocal terms that the *guru* has accepted him wholeheartedly. They also encourage him to be open and sincere in all further talks. At the same time they make it clear that he has much to learn and must therefore give his fullest and deepest attention.

Ashtavakra must have been sorely tempted to ask him, "Who is asking this question? Who wants to know?" But he restrains himself and gives him an answer that would, at that stage, satisfy the disciple. From this simplification of the matter (telling Janaka to cultivate certain "virtues"), you will find that Ashtavakra takes his mature disciple (astonishingly quickly) from this early stage, to the stage at the end where Janaka has the intuitive experience of his subjective identity. Then Janaka exclaims, "Where is the individual? Where is the question of bondage and liberation? Where is the *guru* and where is the disciple?"

Even in the very first words, Ashtavakra gives an amazingly simple formula for being happy in this world. Happiness is important because if you are unhappy in this world, it will be impossible to reach the stage of liberation. In fact, the various qualities or virtues which he has enumerated have an ascending scale leading ultimately to Truth. What Ashtavakra is actually telling his intelligent disciple is that the root of all trouble, that which prevents the seeing of Truth, is desire. Later in the dialogue, he makes it clear that desire in any form is the only obstacle, even if the desire is for liberation! The basis of the desire for liberation is the ignorance about the Truth that there never has been any bondage from which liberation could be desired. Bondage is a concept and therefore liberation is also a concept.

Ashtavakra then proceeds with his answer:

"You are neither earth, nor water, nor fire, nor air, nor space. You are the witness of those five elements as Consciousness. Understanding this is liberation." (3)

Having established a sound working relationship with his disciple, Ashtavakra quickly goes straight to the core of his teaching in this verse, and follows it up at once with the next verse in which he hits his disciple with a "one-two" combination that would have knocked out a disciple of lesser caliber! But Ashtavakra has judged the level of his esteemed disciple accurately. Says Ashtavakra:

"If you detach yourself from the identification with the body and remain relaxed in and as Consciousness, you will, this very moment, be happy, at peace, free from bondage." (4)

This is the very core of the teaching. The rest of the dialogue is merely the expansion of this one essential truth. These two verses must have stunned Janaka into a state of spiritual shock, which was precisely what the sage, as a *guru*, intended to do. He must have realized that Janaka was at a stage of spiritual advancement where a certain block had developed and that block could only be removed by a powerful blasting. The result of this sustained blasting will soon be seen in the sudden transformation which takes place in the disciple at the end of this initial instruction.

There are certain words in these two verses which are most significant in relation to sudden enlightenment which comes about merely through understanding which needs no effort of any kind. Ashtavakra says, through those two verses:

a) You are not the body which is composed of the five elements. You are that Consciousness which has provided the inert body with the sentience that makes the senses function in regard to their objects. It is sentience which makes the psychosomatic apparatus work as a unit.

b) Anticipating the query from his intelligent disciple, the *guru* tells him further, "You" are not the physical organism but Consciousness which works not as someone in charge of the operations of the physical organism but merely as the witness of the operations.

c) You have wrongly identified yourself as the individual, as the doer of all actions that take place through the physical organism, and thereby unnecessarily assume the responsibility for the actions which take place, and thus assume the bondage from which you are seeking liberation.

d) The witness cannot be the doer, and you are therefore not the doer. *With this understanding*, you can detach yourself from the wrong identification with the body. And when you do this, you will automatically assume your true position as the witness and remain relaxed (because there is not the tension of responsibility for the actions) in Consciousness, as Consciousness.

e) Just as sunlight makes objects in a room perceivable but is not concerned with what happens to the objects, it is in Consciousness that all phenomenal objects appear, and such objects are perceived and cognized by Consciousness through the sentient objects, but Consciousness is not involved in what happens to the phenomenal objects, including human beings. Consciousness—the real "you"—merely witnesses all events as in a dream.

f) The state of being disidentified from the body is the state of witnessing (when the individual "me" is not present). And this state of detached witnessing is indeed the state of liberation. This is what the Self-realized *guru* means when he says that when you remain relaxed in Consciousness (without identification with the body), the state of liberation is sudden and immediate.

g) The basis of this concept of sudden enlightenment is the understanding that there cannot exist any individual, as such, because all there is is Consciousness in which appears the totality of phenomenal manifestation, including the individual human beings. The supposed individual has never been under bondage. He thinks he is in bondage only because he has forgotten his original identity as Consciousness-witness, and has falsely identified himself with the physical body.

The words "remain relaxed in Consciousness" form the very basis of the Ashtavakra teaching. He does not prescribe any rigorous set of practices and disciplines. All it needs for enlightenment *to occur* is a clear understanding of a dimension quite different from intellectual comprehension. What intellectual comprehension brings about is a belief in what is comprehended but an intuitive apprehension is based on faith. Intellectual comprehension—belief—is based on argumentation, logic, effort and conflict. Intuitive apprehension—faith—is based on a certain inescapable inevitability, a relaxed acceptance of What-Is, totally free of any doubt or opinion.

At this stage, Ashtavakra wants Janaka to accept his teaching on faith, and he does not put forward arguments to support his statements. "Faith" does not necessarily mean a conflict with reason or a substitute for reason. It merely means not excluding the possibility of the existence of certain levels of reality beyond the pure sense perceptions. Faith is the power which is capable of bringing about the spontaneous apperception of the truth. Faith intuitively recognizes the ring of truth, and opens "the eye of the heart" to apperceive the Truth.

Ashtavakra's confident assertion that enlightenment will occur "this very moment" clearly means this present moment which is the eternal moment when the mind and its conceptualization is totally excluded. As he knows that his disciple is, at that stage, speaking from the body-mind level as an individual, he says "you will, this very moment, be happy, at peace, free from bondage" because that is what he was seeking. What he means is that as soon as there is disidentification with the body, the individual "me" (the ego) will have disappeared, and a stage will have been reached in which the "me" cannot be present as against the "you." This is a stage in which fear and conflict are totally absent—a stage, in other words, of happiness, of peace, of freedom from bondage. Indeed, at the end of Ashtavakra's initial teaching covering the first twenty verses, his royal disciple is shocked out of the complacence of his individuality, and has the actual subjective experience of Unicity, and cannot help bursting out into a song of his spiritual independence. Ashtavakra proceeds:

> *"You do not belong to any caste like Brahmana, nor do you belong to any station in life. You are not the object of any sense. Unattached and formless, you are the witness of the entire universe. Know this, and be happy." (5)*

The traditional four castes in ancient India have been the *Brahmana* (the scholar-priest), the *Kshatriya* (the warrior), the *Vaishya* (the trader), and the *Shudra* (the menial worker). The traditional four stations in life have been *Brahmacharya* (the celibate student), *Grihastha* (householder), *Vanaprastha* (retired from active life), and *Sanyasa* (renunciate from life). Ashtavakra tells Janaka that although as an individual he may be living as a householder belonging to the warrior caste, he truly has neither any caste nor creed. He asks him to see himself not as an individual but as the unattached, formless witness of the entire universe, and as such, no kind of unhappiness can touch him. There is no reason not to be happy in such total freedom, therefore, exhorts Ashtavakra, *be happy*. In other words, the realization of one's true nature is freedom, enlightenment, unalloyed happiness.

> *"Right and wrong, happiness and sorrow are all attributes of the mind, not of You, O all-pervading One. You are neither the doer nor the enjoyer, You who have ever and always been free of all such attachments." (6)*

The question of bondage can never arise in your case because you have never been concerned with any event or any action except as a mere witness. This is what Ashtavakra tells Janaka. In other words, Ashtavakra says that right and wrong, happiness and sorrow are pairs of interdependent opposites without which there cannot be any life in this world. The mind, however, does not accept the polarity, the interdependence of the opposites like beautiful and ugly, good and evil, etc. and thereby creates a dualism and conflict between the opposites.

In each of the initial twenty verses, Ashtavakra states a basic truth. Later on in the dialogue he goes into great detail about these basic truths, but at this stage he is only interested in stating them in order to gauge the reaction of his disciple and to know accurately what course to follow in guiding the disciple. Ashtavakra is at this stage trying to determine the quality and depth of his disciple's receptivity. The entire dialogue is a beautiful example of the practical demonstration of the divine relationship in action at the highest level.

The whole mind that is universal Consciousness gets split or divided when universal Consciousness becomes identified with the psychosomatic organism as a "me" against the "other." The human mind, therefore, being a split-mind can only think in terms of dualism in total forgetfulness of the fact that the basic duality of the observer and the observed in life is polaric. The "me" as the observer cannot exist in the absence of the "other" as the observed object. Each sentient being, each human being, becomes an observed object when another human being is the observer. In other words, every human being is at the same time both observer and observed object, depending on his role at that moment. Both are objects in the totality of the phenomenal manifestation. This truth is realized only when there is detachment from the body-mind organism, only when the observer and the observed object are *both* clearly seen as phenomenal objects even though the observer object assumes the subjectivity of the Noumenon. In other words, when there is detachment, the split-mind gets healed into its original wholeness as the witness.

It is for this reason that the sage Ashtavakra states at the outset that happiness and unhappiness are states of the mind (the split-mind). They do not concern that which you truly are, that is to say, Consciousness operating as the subjective witness of its own objective expression as the phenomenal universe, not involved in any way either with the event or its reaction or its judgment. It is also for this reason that in the very beginning he says, "If you detach yourself from the body..."

The human mind is conditioned to use linear thinking and conscious attention to the utter neglect of the "unconscious." Yet the "unconscious" is capable of a higher wisdom than can be attained by logic. It can see the basic principles, pulses and rhythms of the working of the universe in the unity oneness, which has been described as "a multidimensional network of jewels, each one containing the reflections of the others *ad infinitum*." The human mind seeks what it considers "acceptable" (at that moment) *to the exclusion* of what it then considers "unacceptable." Yet what it seeks is impossible because the opposites cannot exist without each other—they are in a polaric relationship which the Chinese describe as "mutually arising." Being can only come out of nonbeing, light from space, sound from silence, and, therefore, the opposites, although certainly different, are inseparables like the poles of a magnet. This polaric relationship is an explicit duality in which is inherent an implicit unity, and not a dualism. This implicit unity can be experienced only when, as a result of this understanding and the realization of this truth, there is disidentification with the psychosomatic organism as a separate individual entity

Ashtavakra continues:

"You are the one observer and, as such, you have indeed always been free. Your only bondage has been that you see someone else as the observer." (7)

The one observer is, of course, Consciousness—universal Consciousness—in which has appeared, like a network of waves on the ocean, the totality of the phenomenal manifestation. Universal Consciousness, (subjective Noumenon), is therefore the only observer (as pure subjectivity) and everything else in the manifestation is an object. But in life, because of identification with the body, each human being forgets that he is as much of an object as the other objects which he observes. He assumes the subjectivity of the absolute Noumenon, and considers himself the observer of the other observed objects. By so usurping the subjectivity of the one absolute subject, the human being commits the original sin and therefore comes under bondage. In other words, universal Consciousness having conditioned itself as the personal or individual consciousness by identification with a separate entity, considers the person, the limited ego, as the subject observer. As soon as this mistaken identity is realized and the true identity as the one subject—or witness—is established, the bondage disappears, there is enlightenment. In brief, the "me" (in opposition to the "other") disappears and in its place shines the "I" as the one formless eternal subject observer.

Ashtavakra continues:

"You have been bitten by the deadly black serpent of the ego and you therefore consider yourself as the doer. Drink the nectar of the faith that you are not the doer and be happy." (8)

In this verse, Ashtavakra goes to the root of the matter. What is it that is at the root of the concept of bondage and unhappiness? It is the sense of doership, the notion of volition. The entire mechanism of what is known as living one's life is based on the notion that whenever a human being acts in any manner—whatever the act—it is because he wants to act in that manner. In other words, it is supposed that volition is behind every act of a human being and that he is therefore "responsible" for it. The fact of the matter, however, is that human beings usually do not "ace' but "react" to an outside stimulus. If even a little thought is given to the matter, it will be obvious that very few actions are truly the result of volition or acts of will. Most of the time living, for most people, is conditioned by a series of reflexes based essentially on instinct, habit and even propaganda. The scope of deliberate, considered action is in actual life extremely limited. And yet almost every person firmly believes that he is the doer, and that is why Ashtavakra refers to this notion of individual volition as the bite of the deadly serpent of the ego. The sense of doership, the notion of volition is at best only an impulse, a demonstration of the ego, of the "me"-concept. As long as this "condition" remains, so long as there is identification with a phenomenal object as a separate "me", so long must bondage continue.

The only practice which can free man from the poison

of doership is the abandonment of this identification with a particular object as a "me." Such abandonment can only come through the clear and deep understanding—the faith—that volition or sense of doership is merely an inference because there really is no entity to exercise it. Human beings may think that they "live" their lives, but in fact their lives are being lived as part of the total functioning of this entire phenomenal manifestation. All events together constitute the functioning of the manifestation according to the inexorable chain of causation. It would be incredible to imagine that such functioning of totality could leave any room or scope for individual volition, except, of course, as part of that functioning.

It is for this reason that Ashtavakra refers to "faith" as the only remedy for the snake-bite of doership—the faith that the human being exists, not as an individual body/mind entity which is merely a phenomenal object, but as Noumenon, not as an individual object but as the one Subject. Such faith brings about the spontaneous and sudden understanding that "I" am the one subject and the entire phenomenal manifestation is my objective expression. "I" am the universal Consciousness within which has spontaneously arisen the totality of the phenomenal manifestation.

Ashtavakra continues:

"Having burnt down the forest of ignorance with the fire of the conviction 'I am the One, Pure Consciousness', discard all grief and be happy." (9)

"You are that Consciousness—Supreme Bliss— upon which appears this phenomenal manifestation, like the illusion of a snake on a rope. Live happily." (10)

In these two verses, the sage impresses upon his disciple the basic truth that all there is is Consciousness, and therefore there is no question of anyone becoming anything. There is no question of being bound and thereafter being liberated. There is really no question of any "one" being a separate entity, no question of any "object" being this or that, empty or non-empty because it just is not there to have any quality at all. Having said that "You" are—"I" am—the one pure Consciousness, what Ashtavakra emphasizes is the inexistence of any object which, out of ignorance, the disciple considers himself to be. His intention is to return the mind to the source, the Consciousness, and with this aim, he gives the analogy of the illusion of the snake which a piece of rope could give rise to in the dim light. There is a basic imperfection in all analogies like the clay and the pot, or the gold and the ornament, inasmuch as the void is sought to be represented in these analogies by objective images and concepts. But the intention is clear: to stop the mind from objectifying and return it to its true center.

The *guru* is trying to bring about the conviction in his disciple that what he truly is in reality is the subjective, formless Consciousness. This he knows can be done only by eliminating the mistaken identity. The pseudo-subject of pseudo-objects,—the sole factor which obstructs the disciple's realization of his true identity—must be eliminated. Ashtavakra repeats to his disciple that all there is is Consciousness on which spontaneously appears this universe. The universe is only an appearance, an illusion like the snake being mistaken for the rope. Once the mistaken identity is removed, there is nothing to prevent the disciple from being his true identity, and, what is important, living his life from the viewpoint of his true identity, in "silent identification with nonbeing." The conviction about one's true identity, which comes about when the mistaken identity is clearly realized, leads to the kind of living in which personal volition is absent. Then there is full awareness that the human being is "being lived" as an intrinsic part of the totality of functioning in the universe. This is what Ashtavakra means when he says "be happy" or "live happily" because then there is no volition, there is no sense of doership, no sense of guilt or bondage. In other words, living happily means living naturally, living spontaneously, responding to external situations without any planning, without any preconceived notions—in short, without the interference of the mind. Such a response will naturally bring about physical activity but there will be no sense of doership, no illusion of volition, because the physical activity does not involve any mental activation. In short, the response will be spontaneous without volitional interference, and will therefore lead to awakening, to enlightenment. In the absence of volitional involvement, whatever happens is an integral part of the Noumenal functioning, the essence of which is mere witnessing of an event without any judging. Judging presupposes duality, whereas witnessing is beyond duality.

Ashtavakra continues:

"The one who considers himself free is indeed free while the one who considers himself bound remains in bondage. The saying 'As one thinks so one becomes' is certainly a true one." (11)

"The Atman is the sole witness, all pervading, perfect, free Consciousness—actionless, unattached, desireless, at peace with itself. It is only through an illusion that it appears to be involved with the samsara." (12)

In these two verses, Ashtavakra summarizes the position and brings the disciple's attention to the basic truth: all there is is Consciousness—universal Consciousness in which appears the total universe, but which identifies itself with each individual phenomenal object as personal consciousness and thereby comes into *conceptual* bondage. *Atman* or Consciousness, being the only reality, must necessarily be all-pervading and therefore there cannot possibly be any personal, individual entity. But in the duality of the phenomenal appearance, the split mind creates the illusion of "me" and the "other" and thereby also, at the same time, creates the *notion* of bondage. Therefore liberation is only liberation from the concept of bondage, liberation from the operation of the split-mind, liberation from conceptualizing. Let the split-mind stop its conceptualizing and there is no bondage, because in the absence of any mental activity, the split-mind regains its wholeness, its holiness.

What Ashtavakra wants the disciple to understand very clearly is that the entire manifestation—and every object therein that has been given a name, and has some specific significance—is all very much in the mind. Therefore, they do not exist in deep sleep when the mind ceases its conceptualizing. Phenomenal objects including the sky and the sun and the moon, up there or down here or anywhere, simply do not exist except as concepts in the mind, except as illusory appearances in Consciousness, observed and cognized by Consciousness.

Again and again, in these twenty verses, Ashtavakra does his best to put into words what truly cannot be put into words. He does this for only one reason, and that is that he hopes that there will be perhaps a single word or a single sentence that may reveal the truth and remove the obfuscation that has appeared on the disciple's real nature. He repeatedly avers that all there is is Consciousness and that therefore the disciple, like the *guru* cannot possibly be anything but Consciousness; further that all phenomenal objects—including the *guru* and the disciple—are nothing but the subjective Noumenon in its objective expression as the manifestation. But the realization of this truth at the intellectual level is just not sufficient because at the root of the intellectual comprehension the culprit is still there as the individual comprehender! The individual outside crust has to be shattered before the intellectual comprehension can be transformed into intuitive apprehension or apperception. And this individual crust can be shattered only by the disidentifying of the pseudo-subjectivity through a subjective experience of the sheer absence of a separate individual entity.

Having stated in unequivocal terms the Truth, the *guru* urges the disciple in the following verses to go deeper than the intellectual level and to abide in the Truth:

"Give up the illusion that you are the individual self together with all external and internal self-modifications, and meditate on the Atman, the immutable, non-dual Consciousness." (13)

"Dear child, long have you been caught in the bonds of identification with the body. Sever it with the sword of Knowledge, and be happy." (14)

"You are unattached, actionless, self-effulgent, without blemish. This indeed is your bondage, that you practice meditation." (15)

This is a very important set of verses for several reasons. To begin with, the *guru* here acknowledges the fact that all he can do is to point to the Truth. He cannot hand over enlightenment as a gift on a platter to the disciple. So long as the identification with a body-mind organism as a separate individual entity continues, the identified pseudo-subject must remain in bondage. Apart from stating the Truth as clearly as possible—after "showing your true nature as if in a mirror", as Nisargadatta Maharaj used to say— there is nothing more that the *guru* can do. He can only wait for the disciple to receive and absorb the Truth. The problem is made immensely more difficult by the fact that there is precious little that the disciple himself can "do" in a positive way. Indeed, this is what Ashtavakra indicates to Janaka when he says that practicing meditation is itself bondage!

What is necessary for the disidentification to take place is the abandonment of the phenomenal object in which the subject is centered. Any positive action can only be on the part of the same *phenomenal* center, the same ego which is to be dropped. What is (in fact) necessary is non-action leaving the *Noumenal* center in charge, free from any interference from the split-mind and its creation, the ego. Such non-action can come only as a spontaneous arising or consequence of a very deep, intense realization of the Truth, without the slightest interference by way of mental activity. Indeed such a transformation, such a disidentification, cannot be brought about. *It can only happen.* This is so because such a transformation presupposes the total absence of the illusory doer: The "doer" is indeed the obstruction, the bondage which is to be cut asunder by the word of Knowledge. It is a deep intuitive understanding in which the comprehender (the split-mind, the ego) is absent. This "happening" is not in the hands of either the individual *guru* or the individual disciple. It can occur only at the appropriate time and place in the totality of functioning when the divine relationship between the *guru* as Consciousness and the disciple as Consciousness is ripe enough to fructify, when the *guru* and the disciple meet face to face like two mirror surfaces facing each other.

It is for this reason that Ashtavakra asks his royal disciple to "give up the illusion that you are the individual self" and "meditate" on the fact that "you are the *Atman*, the immutable non-dual Consciousness." The word "meditate" in verse 13 and verse 15 are used to express what would *appear* to be contradictory instructions. But this is not so. Indeed, it is just this subtle difference which makes the difference between success and failure for the disciple. In the earlier verse, the word "meditate" is used precisely to denote the "non-action" that could produce the awakening to enlightenment. Ashtavakra urges his disciple to realize his identity as the non-dual Consciousness and to remain in that realization in which the split-mind is totally absent. In such meditation, there is no ego present as the meditator. There is only the realization of the identity as the non-dual Consciousness.

When Ashtavakra says in verse 15 that practicing meditation is the very bondage from which liberation is sought, the meaning is clear that such meditation presupposes the deliberate action of the ego as the meditator, practicing meditation, with the specific intention of realizing something. And whatever the ego does is creating further cords of bondage. The point is simple. The basic Truth is that the true nature of all sentient beings is pure Consciousness which is the substance of all phenomenal appearances. If this is accepted—and it must be—then anyone wanting to "do" something, in order to "become" enlightened, is surely turning his back on the basic Truth. Any positive action in order to become enlightened presupposes the existence of an individual entity whereas "enlightenment" is itself the state in which no separate individual can exist. It is for this reason that Ashtavakra calls the *practicing of meditation* the very bondage from which liberation is sought. In other words, it is only non-volitional motiveless functioning that can lead to the awakening to enlightenment. Any sort of intentional action by way of discipline or practice would necessarily be an insurmountable obstacle to such awakening.

Ashtavakra continues to encourage his disciple towards his awakening:

"It is you who pervade this universe, and this universe exists in you. You are truly pure Consciousness by nature. Be not petty-minded." (16)

When you are the whole manifestation, says Ashtavakra, why identify yourself with an infinitesimally small, paltry part of it—like an individual—why be so petty-minded? In this verse, the sage also makes it clear that there is no phenomenon without Noumenon, and no Noumenon without phenomenon, because without the subject there cannot be any objects, and without objects the question of the subject does not arise. He tells his disciple not to make *any basic* distinction between the Absolute and the manifested world: you pervade this universe, and this universe exists in you. Ashtavakra, at the end of his initial instruction, is compressing it in as few words as possible so that it may pierce his disciple's spiritual heart like an arrow. In effect he is saying that on seeing one thing you see all: that is to say, that phenomenon and Noumenon are one, although *notionally* they may be differentiated as appearance and its source.

"Abide in that Consciousness which you are— unconditioned, immutable, formless, serene and imperturbable, of unfathomable intelligence." (17)

Ashtavakra concludes this instruction with the three closing stanzas:

"Know that which has form to be unreal and the formless to be the real. Having understood this principle, there will be no possibility of rebirth." (18)

To the very last of this initiation, Ashtavakra enunciates one aspect of the Truth after another in different words from different angles because the disciple has yet to expose his own level of understanding and capacity

What he stresses here is the important fact that anything that has form must necessarily be an appearance and therefore subject to change and final dissolution. This automatically means that what is real is the formless which is invulnerable, not subject either to change or death. Ashtavakra is saying that what we truly are is the timeless, spaceless, formless immutable Noumenon. What we appear to be as separate objects are temporal, finite and sensorially perceptible phenomena.

Ashtavakra goes on to say that all phenomena are *basically* without existence, that is to say, appearances subject to change and decay. What you are is the immutable Noumenon. Once this truth has been accepted without any mental reservation, then the question of re-birth is irrelevant. But, if you cannot get rid of the identification with a separate individual phenomenal object and continue to think that you are that object, then you as that object will be liable to suffer pleasure and pain both in this life and in the next and the next until in the spiritual evolution you awake to this true principle.

There is one other point which the sage suggests in these lines: the form is an appearance, a presence which is subject to change and decay; therefore its source must necessarily be formless, an absence from which must arise the presence of the appearance. And yet both the presence and the absence are concepts which depend upon a supposed entity conceiving the concepts. There is neither presence nor absence in deep sleep because there is no entity conceiving any objects. To get at the source (even this is a concept!), therefore, what is necessary is the withdrawal of the conceiving entity.

This is the aspect of the matter which the sage highlights in the next verse:

"Just as the surface of a mirror exists within and without the image reflected in the mirror, so also the Supreme Self exists both within and without the physical body." (19)

Ashtavakra points out in this important verse that what we Noumenally are is definitely not a thing or an object—which the personal pronoun cannot help suggesting—but more of a process or a background, like the screen on which a movie is seen. In the absence of the background there could be no appearance at all, although in the case of the phenomenal manifestation, the background— Consciousness—is itself responsible for and constitutes the appearance. The point is that unless there is total "withdrawal" into impersonality, the consideration of "who (or what) am I" may mean in effect too simple a transference from phenomenality to Noumenality. It would not have the strength to break the conditioning brought about by the notion of identity leading to the supposed bondage. It is only a direct withdrawal into impersonality that is more likely to bring about the startling transformation known as *metanoesis,* whereby there is a sudden and immediate conviction that the identification with a separate individual entity never did really exist and was essentially nothing but an illusion.

Perhaps it is for this reason that Ashtavakra suggests the mirror simile for Consciousness which reflects everything, retains nothing and in itself has no perceptible existence. That is to say, Consciousness is the background of what we appear to be as phenomenal objects, and yet it is not anything objective. Just as the reflection in the mirror is a mere appearance without any existence and the mirror is the one which has existence but is not affected in any way by the reflection, so also the psychosomatic apparatus, being only an appearance in Consciousness, has no independent existence. The Consciousness in which it appears is not affected in any way by the appearance of the objects therein.

Ashtavakra in this verse brings out the transcendence aspect of the unmanifest absolute in relation to the image or appearance of the manifest phenomena. In the next and final stanza, he emphasizes the immanence aspect of the

Noumenon in relation to the phenomena.

> *"Just as the all-pervading space is both inside and outside the pot, so also the eternal and all-pervading Consciousness is immanent in all beings and objects." (20)*

The boundary of the pot may appear to condition and limit the space within the pot but in fact space, as such, cannot be conditioned by the pot which itself exists in space. Similarly, although the universal Consciousness may appear to be conditioned by the individual psychosomatic apparatus, all phenomenal objects are merely appearances in Consciousness. All there is is Consciousness, immanent in everything phenomenal, inasmuch as there cannot be any phenomena without Consciousness. In this concluding verse, Ashtavakra brings out the importance of emphasizing the ground—the background and the immanence—rather than the personal element so that the final spotlight is not so much on the true nature of the self but more on the withdrawal into impersonality. Instead of saying that "your" true nature is Consciousness, he says that all there is, within and without all phenomena, is Consciousness.

CHAPTER TWO

✢

The bold statement of the spiritual fact—the Truth—
enunciated by Ashtavakra in the first twenty verses, without
the slightest attempt to defend or justify what he had said,
could have had various reactions at the intellectual level:

a) one of direct opposition, almost a confrontation;

b) one of skepticism based on the feeling "well, if you
say so...";

c) one of mere abject surrender by the disciple;

d) an acceptance of defeat on the basis "seems all
right, I can't find a fault with it."

Or, there could be a reaction at a totally different level,
in a totally different dimension, a direct hit to the heart,
"a gut-feeling" not to be denied. Ashtavakra must have
been hoping for such a reaction from Janaka, and as the
guru, he must have felt much gratification when Janaka
spontaneously and explosively burst out:

*"I really am the taintless, serene pure Consciousness,
quite apart from the phenomenal universe. How
long have I been unnecessarily bewildered by
illusion!" (21)*

The *guru*'s announcement made such an impact on the disciple who was just about ripe and ready for that spark of wisdom that he bursts out into an exclamation of ecstatic delight. The walls of the prison within which he had felt himself imprisoned for a series of lifetimes had suddenly been pulled down and there was an extraordinary feeling of total freedom. For the *guru*'s words to have such an electric effect, the disciple must listen with an alertness of mind combined with a kind of receptivity that will not be blocked by the conceptualizing interference of the split-mind. He must also have the courage to let the heart prevail over the head, to not let logic and reason block the spontaneous wisdom of natural inherent intuition. The ripe and ready disciple with this kind of receptivity receives his *guru*'s wisdom with an ease and effortlessness that astonishes himself and others. Whenever Nisargadatta Maharaj was requested by a disciple for his "grace", he invariably used to say, "My grace is always there for the asking, but are you ready to accept it?"

Janaka continues:

"As I Myself illumine this body, so also do I reveal this whole universe. Therefore, the entire universe is Mine alone, or else nothing is mine." (22)

Janaka's entire answer (consisting of twenty-four verses) to Ashtavakra's opening address shows quite clearly the depth to which his immediate understanding has reached. Indeed, what Ashtavakra had promised by way of sudden enlightenment, if the identification with the body is dropped, has indeed happened in the case of Janaka. The ceding of the personal, individual identification as a separate entity has suddenly brought about the withdrawal into impersonality, which in its turn means identity with Noumenality. Janaka, in other words, realizes that there is really no "me" to own anything because the individual does not at all exist apart from the total manifestation. In fact the individual is part of the manifestation, and, when in deep sleep there is no awareness of the manifested universe, there is no awareness of the "me" either: the manifestation and the individual "me" therein both appear and disappear together.

Janaka has suddenly realized his Noumenality, but in the phenomenal sense; otherwise there would be no awareness of "I." Noumenality cannot know "I" because in Noumenality there is no duality of the knower and the known. Therefore, phenomenally speaking, what he says is that all objects, all bodies, constituting the universe, can appear to exist only when "my" radiance falls upon them. Therefore he owns the entire universe. On the other hand, he says, "I" can shine only when I touch them with my radiance: "the entire universe is mine alone, or else nothing is mine." Without the Noumenon, the phenomena cannot appear because it is the Noumenal light which illumines them. And unless the phenomena are seen, the Noumenon cannot be known. Indeed, what Janaka has experienced is that the Noumenon and the phenomena are not two but one. The "me" in Janaka has experienced the "I", and "he" has become liberated! The universal Consciousness which had identified itself with the individual Janaka has shed its identification and has suddenly recovered its universality!

Janaka continues:

"On renouncing the body along with the rest of the manifestation, there has been, as if by magic, a perception of the supreme Self." (23)

Janaka has suddenly realized that there is no question of acquiring a thing known as liberation or enlightenment. He realizes that the surrender of identification as a separate entity is all that is necessary for immediate realization of the reality. This idea he expands in the verses that follow.

"Just as waves, foam and bubbles are not different

from the water, so also the phenomenal universe appearing in Consciousness is not different from it." (24)

"Just as cloth, after an analysis is found to be nothing other than thread, similarly the phenomenal manifestation of the universe is found, on intelligent perception, to be nothing other than Consciousness." (25)

"Just as sugar made from sugar-cane juice is wholly pervaded by the sugar-cane juice, so also the phenomenal universe which is produced within Me is wholly pervaded by Me." (26)

In these verses, Janaka expresses his subjective experience of the "I"—feeling, according to which he feels the oneness of the Noumenon and the phenomena, the immanence of the Noumenon in all phenomenal objects and therefore the impossibility of the existence of a human being with independence and autonomy. The Noumenon and the phenomenal manifestation and everything therein are all one.

"It is through ignorance of the Atman that the phenomenal universe appears to be real, and this illusion disappears with the realization of one's true nature, just as the illusion of the snake appears through the ignorance of the object being a rope, and disappears after the recognition of the rope as a rope." (27)

"Light is my very nature. Indeed, I am Light, and none other. It is indeed "I" that shine when the universe manifests itself." (28)

Janaka's understanding of his own beingness as Light must have enormously pleased Ashtavakra because the shining of the Noumenon and the seeing of the phenomena is a simultaneous happening, and this Janaka has intuitively apperceived. Janaka says "it is indeed I that shine when the universe manifests itself", because, as the Taoist says, "I am the light that falls on ten thousand specks of dust (manifested phenomena) so that each may shine." For instance, in the "darkness" of deep sleep, the phenomena are unseen because "I" as Consciousness do not shine and I remain as unseen Light. Only when one awakens from deep sleep, one's radiance falls upon the phenomena and they reappear. Phenomenal objects, therefore, cannot be anything other than "my" shining: without me (as "I") the objects cannot appear, and without the objects "I" cannot be known—phenomena are the objective expression of the subjective "I."

The same idea is further developed in the following verses:

"The arising of the phenomenal universe which appears in Me gives the impression of being real because of ignorance, just as the mother of pearl gives the impression of silver, the rope that of the snake, and the rays of the sun that of water in a mirage." (29)

"Just as a pot dissolves into clay, a wave into water, or a bracelet into gold, so also the phenomenal universe which has arisen in Me will also dissolve into Me." (30)

The point that is being made in these verses is that at no point of time did the silver and the snake and the water in the mirage really exist. It did not exist, of course, when the ignorance was destroyed by knowledge of the truth, but even during the existence of the illusion, all that existed was the mother of pearl, the rope and the rays of the sun. There always was only one reality, before the illusion, during the illusion and after the illusion. In other words, all that happened was that the reality was discovered when the cause of the illusion—the ignorance—was removed.

Every thing or object in the manifested universe is a product of Consciousness, both during the illusion when the manifestation appeared to be "real" and after the realization of the Truth as in the case of Janaka. We are nothing but Consciousness, and never have been anything else. Perhaps it would be easier to "understand" the Truth if it is conceived that there never has been any "we" at any time, and that all there is—and has ever been—is Consciousness. "We" think of ourselves, consciously or unconsciously, as sentient beings and therefore as separate from the manifestation: "we" are the subject and the rest of the manifestation is the object. The reality is that "we", as manifested phenomena, are actually nothing but a part of the one manifested universe. What makes us think of ourselves as separate is the fact that the apparent universe becomes *known* to us, as sentient beings, through sentience operating through cognitive faculties. This "sentience", as an aspect of Consciousness in *itself*, is a direct manifestation of the whole-mind. And it is for this reason that we cannot get rid of the deepest feeling that "I" am other than the manifested appearance. And so indeed we are, but the illusion (the *maya*) consists in the fact that instead of *collectively* considering ourselves as sentience which enables us to cognize the manifestation (including sentient beings) which has appeared in Consciousness, we consider ourselves as *separate* individual entities. And therein lies our suffering and bondage. As soon as there is realization (awakening to the fact) that we are not separate entities but Consciousness itself (with sentience acting as the means for cognizing the manifestation), the illusion of separateness—the cause of our suffering and bondage—disappears. There is then the clear apperception that unmanifested, we are Noumenon whilst manifested, we are appearance; no more separate than substance and its form (gold and the gold ornament). Manifestation arises from the unmanifest and in due course sinks back into the unmanifest. The human beings as *individuals* are *really* quite irrelevant, except, of course, as illusory characters in a dream play which is known as "life."

Janaka continues to express the joy of Self-realization:

"0, the wonder that I am! I salute Myself who knows no decay and survives even the destruction of the entire universe from the creator Brahma to a blade of grass." (31)

"0, the wonder that I am! I salute myself who, though with a body, am one who neither goes anywhere nor comes from anywhere but ever abides pervading the universe." (32)

"0, the wonder that I am! I salute myself, none more capable, who is bearing the burden o f the entire universe without even touching it with my body." (33)

"0, the wonder that I am! I salute myself who has nothing or everything that is accessible to thought and word." (34)

These four verses constitute a sort of hymn to the Self, based on the conceptual mechanism of the appearance of the manifestation of the universe. The process of phenomenality is simple enough! When there is a movement in the Consciousness-at-rest, Noumenon – which is not aware of itself – it becomes suddenly aware of itself, aware of its presence as I Am, and simultaneously, there is a spontaneous arising of the phenomenal manifestation. "We" are only a small intrinsic part of the total phenomenal manifestation, and, therefore, in the objective sense, there is no real difference between animate and inanimate objects. The apparent difference is in subjectivity inasmuch as sentience, an aspect of the non-apparent Consciousness, arises independently of the objective manifestation in order that phenomena may be cognized as such. In other words, "we" are merely objects, through which Consciousness cognizes objects by means of sentience. Also "we" are the instruments through which the functioning of the universe takes place, although, mistakenly we think we live our lives!

In these four verses, Janaka expresses the essential understanding which has suddenly dawned on him, that everything that is perceptible to the senses can only be an appearance in mind (which is the content of Consciousness) and therefore cannot have any other kind of existence. Even more importantly, this "mind" itself cannot exist independently for the simple reason that it is merely a symbol for what we ourselves are, and thus cannot possibly be an object to be cognized. Indeed, Janaka has "magically" realized that "I" is verily the mind and the Consciousness, and that the phenomenal manifestation is merely the objective expression of the subjective, unmanifest "I."

Janaka's understanding thus extends to the fact that What-We-Are is Noumenon—timeless, spaceless and not perceptible to the senses, while what we *appear* to be (as separate objects) are phenomena—limited by time and space, and perceptible to the senses. Furthermore, he also intuitively now understands that phenomena are merely appearances in Consciousness and therefore illusory, but that they are in reality nothing but Noumenon in manifestation—in other words, that the only way in which Noumenon can be known is as phenomena.

What is most important, however, in the case of Janaka

in this moment of Self-realization, is that a sudden adjustment has taken place, a sudden displacement of subjectivity has occurred from phenomenon to Noumenon, from individual personality to impersonality, from identity with a supposed individual to identity with the universal Absolute—in short from a phenomenal "me" to the Noumenal "I." The result is that all questions and problems, including those concerning suffering and bondage which affect only the "me" have therefore disappeared along with the disappearance of the phenomenal "me."

"Knowledge, the knower and that which is to be known, as the triad, do not really exist in reality. I am that stainless Consciousness in which this triad appears through ignorance." (35)

In this verse, Janaka emphasizes the fact that all relative knowledge depends upon the split-mind whereas he himself, as "I," the whole-mind of universal Consciousness, transcends the split-mind of relativity. He is aware that phenomenal life in the relativity of the apparent universe means for the ordinary man nothing but objectivization, a continuous process—except in deep sleep— of objectifying. He therefore says that what he is—what every human being is—is that Consciousness in which this objectivization takes place. He, in effect, reminds himself that objectivization is precisely the obstruction to the apperceiving of what we truly Are. In other words, if we stopped thinking (other than of what we are doing at that moment), or conceptualizing, or fabricating objects in mind, we would automatically remain in wholemind, not involved in relative duality.

This is the point he pursues in the next three verses:

"0, the root o f misery is indeed in dualism. There is no remedy for it other than the realization that all objects of experience are unreal, and that I am the one pure Consciousness." (36)

"I am the pure Consciousness but I have, through ignorance imposed limitations upon myself. With

this constant conviction, I abide in the Consciousness without any conceptualizing." (37)

"The illusion of bondage and liberation, having lost its basic support (of ignorance) remains no longer. 0, the universe has emanated from me but it is not within me." (38)

These three verses provide an extraordinary summary of Ashtavakra's teaching which the disciple has so thoroughly and deeply absorbed.

Janaka recognizes dualism as the root of misery. "I" is universal or impersonal Consciousness, the whole-mind which is not affected by the appearance within it of the phenomena. When the impersonal Consciousness turns outward and objectifies, it must divide itself into a duality of a subject and its object. Indeed the process of objectifying is by splitting the whole-mind—the "I"—into a subject and object. The wholeness of pure subjectivity thus loses its equanimity and gets split into contrasting elements of positive and negative, love and hate, pleasure and pain etc. through the duality of subject and object. The *phenomenal* subject and its object are both objects in the manifestation, but this subject as the "me" (the universal Consciousness identified with each object) considers itself as a separate entity in dualism but, being essentially an object, it suffers the experience of pain and pleasure. Noumenally, however, there is only pure subjectivity and there is no object to suffer. This objectivizing of pure subjectivity is precisely what is known as bondage, and the disidentification with a separate entity and withdrawing back in impersonality is precisely what is known as liberation. Indeed, this disidentification, as Janaka asserts, is the only remedy for the misery of bondage.

As soon as there is realization of the whole conceptual structure of the phenomenal universe and the role of the individual sentient being, as soon as the conceptual structure is seen in true perspective, it must collapse along with the twin concepts of bondage and enlightenment.

What precisely is to be "known?" Only that the *appearance* of the phenomenal universe is the objective expression of the Noumenon. Such appearance necessitates the conceptual appearance of space and time so that phenomenal objects can be extended in order to be cognized. Therefore, phenomena are the *appearance* of Noumenon and not something separately projected by Noumenon. Like all phenomena, "we" have no nature of our own other than as the functioning of Noumenon. As Noumenon, "we" can neither be bound nor liberated.

> *"I am now convinced that the whole universe, including this body, is without substance and that what I am is pure Consciousness. So what basis can conceptualization now have?" (39)*

> *"Body, heaven and hell, bondage and freedom, as also fear, all these are mere concepts. What have I to do with all these, I who am pure Consciousness?" (40)*

> *"0, there is absolutely no dualism for me. Even in the midst of people I feel as if I am alone. To what should I attach myself?" (41)*

> *"I am not this body, nor do I have any body because I am not a separate individual but pure*

*Consciousness. My only bondage was that I had a
zest for life."* (42)

In these four verses, Janaka proclaims total
disidentification with any psychosomatic apparatus as
a separate individual. Therefore, since the very basis of
conceptualization is gone, objectivization has ceased, and
a non-objective relationship arisen. In other words, Janaka
finds that he does not think of himself as an object at
all—any kind of object, either physical or psychic—and
therefore finds himself without any objective quality
whatsoever. He is free of the very idea—neither the presence
nor the absence of anything perceptible or conceivable. This
has led him to a non-objective relationship with others
inasmuch as he no longer regards other objects—animate
or inanimate—as his objects. Thus, Janaka *now* sees both
supposed subject ("me") and its supposed objects as mere
appearances. This understanding, this intuitive conviction,
is that *as objects* we are *all* mere appearances without any
substance as phenomena, but that, as Noumenon, what we
all are cannot be anything different. This means in effect
sudden enlightenment, the instant elimination of what is
metaphysically considered as "ignorance."

Duality has been accepted as part of the mechanism of
manifestation, while the dualism of "me" as the pseudo-
subject against the "other" as the object, has disappeared.

It is perhaps necessary to add that in a non-objective
relationship like this, there is really no "love" intrinsic in
it. "Love"—as the word is generally understood—denotes
separation, whereas a non-objective relationship means not
"love" but compassion or *karuna*. The essence of this is
immediate joy, being at-one-ment. We do not "love" others,
we *are* others.

What Janaka also points out is that this basic
understanding brings out the undeniable fact that, other
than this clear apperception that the primal substance of all

sentient (and insentient) beings is the same Noumenon, there cannot be any action, any effort, that can lead an individual to his "enlightenment." This is so because such belief is based on the concept that there is a "he" to be enlightened, whereas "enlightenment" merely denotes a state of beingness where no separate individual can exist. Any action, any practice is phenomenal, and it is obvious that a phenomenon cannot act upon Noumenon—a shadow cannot act upon its substance. In other words, any *intentional* procedure, practice or action of any kind is a definite obstruction to what is known as awakening or illumination or enlightenment. This is because any intentional deed is based on the superstition that an individual exists. Enlightenment is the name given to the Noumenal state. How can a phenomenal object be enlightened?!

Perhaps the error has arisen because of a confusion between what is understood by the word "awakening" and the effect of such awakening which may be understood by the word "deliverance." "Awakening" is what has happened to Janaka on listening to Ashtavakra's words: a sudden coincidence of intellectual comprehension and intuitive apprehension, wherein the relative split of the mind into subject and object is suddenly healed into its original wholeness, thereby causing an immediate timelessness through an instantaneous break in the succession of duration. This clearly means that no action or process, the basis of which is duration, could possibly bring about a sudden suspension or break in its own temporal functioning.

It is the *guru* who acts as the catalyst which brings about the necessary healing of the split-mind through an immediate intemporal intervention at an appropriate moment when "a solution of successional continuity is presented." And it is obvious that such an appropriate moment could not possibly be created volitionally in the context of spatial duration. Such an appropriate moment can only *occur* as a part of the Noumenal functioning of totality, only when the very happening of "enlightenment" is appropriate as part of the What-Is at that *kshana* or split-second.

Non-objective relationship brings about, through its very nature, two developments:

a) conceptualization ceases

b) life is lived spontaneously without volition

This is what Janaka says in these verses. He has apperceived what Ashtavakra meant to tell him—that conceptualizing or objectivizing is what prevents us from apperceiving What-We-Truly-Are. If we cease fabricating objects in mind, we will stop perceiving what we are not, and apperceive What-We-Are. Such apperceiving of What-We-Are is just the enlightenment that is sought. It is the awakening from the dream of an objective universe to the Noumenal actuality of What-Is, which is prior to all thought, all conceptualization. Briefly, all that Ashtavakra said—and Janaka apperceived—is that as long as we are conceptualizing we put ourselves "out" of our Noumenality, and as soon as we stop conceptualizing we are "in" Noumenality. Having said this—and even this saying is conceptualizing!—it may be added that conceptualizing is not the sort of obstacle that needs a substitute or a counter-force to knock it out. Indeed, any positive action can only strengthen the obstacle because the obstacle arose in the first place because of the positive action of conceptualizing—the stopping of conceptualizing is all the action, a sort of negative action, that is necessary.

The foundation on which all conceptualizing is based is the fallacious identification of What-I-Am (which is subjectivity) with what-I-appear-to-be as an object. It is the supposed separate entity "me" which assumes the responsibility (and the consequent misery and unhappiness) of doership. If this false identity is given up, the very basis of conceptualization will have been demolished. How, then, as Janaka says, can conceptualization take place when it has lost its basic support? The apparent difficulty of disidentification is that we are indeed *sentience*, the subjective faculty, the "I", but we forget the sentient element as the sentient being and identify ourselves with the *individual* being. All that is necessary is to understand the situation as it prevails. Observe the false identification at least intellectually, in the beginning. When such intellectual reasoning (the dialectic understanding), goes deeper and deeper and reaches the stage of absolute conviction, it causes a withdrawal into impersonality, a definite loosening of the false identification. It brings about a conceptual negativity which creates a set of conditions for the final annihilation of the "me" and the *occurrence* of what is termed "awakening" or "enlightenment" or whatever. You could, if you prefer, call this process an "effort", but the point is that this process itself is necessarily a negative sort of process. It means merely understanding the situation. It is not the positive effort of an "individual" with the *deliberate intention* of bringing about a positive result. All that happens is that intellectual or dialectic understanding, when it is allowed to function, gradually turns into conviction. This in turn creates the necessary psychosomatic condition for Noumenal understanding to occur suddenly at an appropriate time, in appropriate circumstances. The split-mind regains its wholeness and holiness.

Such a sudden transformation—the metanoesis—known by various names such as the awakening or enlightenment, means in effect, subjective experience of the "I-feeling." It is this subjective experience which Janaka expresses in the final three verses of his immediate reaction to his *guru*'s initial instruction. The disidentification with the body has brought about the demolition of the "me" and with it the desire, the volition, the zest for life. So, says Janaka, when there is no more desire and zest for life, the very foundation and basis of the conceptual bondage has been cracked.

"O, in Me, the limitless ocean, the movement in the mind has produced the many worlds like the wind

produces diverse waves on the ocean." (43)

"In Me, the limitless ocean, when the wind subsides and the mind becomes quiet, unfortunately for the trader in the form of the individual person, the ship of the conceptualized universe sinks." (44)

"How remarkable! In Me, the limitless ocean, the waves of individual selves arise according to their inherent nature, meet and play with one another for a while and then disappear." (45)

In those three verses, Janaka clearly shows that he has withdrawn into impersonality, and in a non-objective relationship, he sees the universe as a spontaneous arising in Consciousness. In the subjective "I" (Noumenal potentiality), arises the actuality of the phenomenal universe including the sentient beings which appear and disappear as integral parts of phenomenality.

All these verses clearly indicate, as almost every Master has unequivocally declared, that no object has any self-nature, that an object lacks objective existence. What this means is that all any object is, is the apparent perceiving of it. It has no nature *of its own*. It is merely an appearance like the wave on the surface of the ocean.

Once there is conviction that I, as the phenomenal "me", is only what is perceived and interpreted by another phenomenal object, the "me", as the particular phenomenal object, will act according to its inherent tendencies (conditioned by the environment) because it has no independent nature of its own. In other words, there would, when the understanding is put into practice, be no "subject", no "do-er", to be responsible for the action. If there is perfect understanding, there cannot in practice be anything other than mere witnessing (without judging) of all actions that happen through the instrumentation of that particular body-mind apparatus. In the absence of the "me", all action becomes spontaneous, natural, Noumenal, a part of the functioning of totality. The dual character of the subjective "I" functioning through the psychosomatic apparatus of the "me" is clearly recognized, so that the pseudo-subjectivity of the "me" cannot prevail. The "me" is seen as the peg (that it is) on which each observer hangs his impressions of that moment, whether sincere or otherwise. It is most important to note that the understanding comports the dual character of the Noumenal "I" functioning through the phenomenal "me." Such *duality* is clearly recognized as only being a mechanism for totality to function as the observer-object and the observed-object. It is totally different from the *dualism* between "me" and the "other" which is the very basis of the conceptual bondage. The ultimate truth is that "I" that is subjectively and necessarily devoid of plurality. It is only as a concept that I can appear as "singular." This in effect means that bondage and entitification are one and the same phenomenon. More importantly, in the absence of an entity, there is no "me" to "do" anything whatever.

Of course, the apparent phenomenal universe is dependent on apparent action. "Our living" (truly our "being lived") is this apparent functioning. This is why the Buddha was supposed to have "preached for 49 years but no word passed his lips", and the sage Vasishtha was supposed to be "a *nitya brahmachari* (a confirmed celibate) when he was the father of a hundred children."

While Ashtavakra must have felt extremely gratified with the spontaneous response from his mature disciple, he knows that it is the application of these doctrines to daily life which is relevant and important. Therefore, in the verses which follow, Ashtavakra impresses upon Janaka the need to find out if he has in fact applied the knowledge to his daily living, whether he has actually faced the fact that he does not—and cannot—exist as an entity. In a series of fourteen verses, Ashtavakra asks Janaka to test himself in various ways to find out whether he has in fact truly learned his lesson or whether he has merely parroted his *guru*'s words. He wants Janaka himself to find out.

CHAPTER THREE

In the following fourteen verses, Ashtavakra tests the genuineness, or otherwise, of Janaka's self-proclaimed awakening. He points to Janaka's daily life as a king and ruler, and brings out various instances which could be interpreted as serious lacunae in the life and behavior of a person who is supposedly a liberated person, and places Janaka in a position where he must explain his attitude to life. In other words, Ashtavakra becomes the devil's advocate in order to find out if his disciple has truly understood his teaching in all its subtleties and apparent contradictions.

"How is it that having understood your true nature as the serene indestructible One, you continue to be attached to the acquisition of wealth?" (46)

"Attachment to the illusory objects of senses arises out of ignorance of the Self, just as greed for silver arises from the illusion created by the mother of pearl." (47)

"Having known that you are That in which arises the phenomenal universe like waves on the ocean, why do you run about like a wretched being?" (48)

"Having heard one's identity as the incomparably beautiful Noumenon, how is it possible for one to continue to be attracted to sensual objects and thus debase oneself?" (49)

It is indeed strange that the sense of "mine-ness" should continue to prevail in a sage who has realized the Self in all beings and all beings in the Self." (50)

"It is indeed strange that one abiding in the supreme transcendent non-duality, and intent on liberation, should be subject to lust and weakened by amorous activities.„ (51)

"It is a strange fact of this world that a man, physically weak and obviously at the end of his life, should lust for sensual pleasure even after being aware that lust is an enemy of knowledge." (52)

In these seven verses, Ashtavakra accuses Janaka of being still attached to sensual pleasures; now in the following verses, he proceeds to test Janaka in other areas of life.

"It is strange that one who is supposed to have developed dispassion towards this world and the next, who is supposed to be able to discriminate between the intransient and the transient, and is in search of emancipation, should yet fear the dissolution of the body." (53)

This is an important verse bringing out the strength of the ego and the entity. Ashtavakra uses the same word *moksha* both for "emancipation" and "the dissolution of the body", suggesting that there cannot be emancipation without a disidentification from the body. In fact, the identification with the body as the ego is so strong that people accept the idea of the dissolution of the body as inevitable but want the separate identity to continue even with another body. Hence, the persistent interest in rebirth, the soul, and the question of what happens after death.

There is a great deal of misconception about the matter of death, and Ashtavakra implies in this verse that those who can discriminate between the intransient and the transient should not be under any such misconception. Life and death are both concepts, one being the absence of the other. There is nothing-no thing-like darkness which is only the absence of light. Death is only apparent absence of life, and as such there is no thing like death. Life itself is merely a concept extended in space-time, and so therefore is death. There is a phenomenal manifestation of "live-ing" and "*die-ing*" but there cannot be any factual entity as the live-er of life or a die-er of death. What-We-Are (Consciousness) is manifested in space/time as an appearance of "live-ing" and the functioning of all such appearances constitutes what we call "life", itself a concept. This appearance of "live-ing" disappears in that of "*die-ing*" but the understanding of the basic difference between intransience and transience must include the fact that What-We-Are can neither "live" nor "die." The jnani ignores the transient concepts of both living and dying and inheres in the Noumenal presence which we all are. In brief, what can die? Only that which is born. What is born? Only "matter." Therefore, it is only "matter" which can be born and which will die.

> "*Whether he is feted and feasted, or pestered and annoyed, the serene one, with the perception of the Self, is neither gratified nor upset.*" (54)

> "*The wise one witnesses the actions of his own body as if he is witnessing those of another body. How*

then can he be affected by praise or blame?" (55)

"How can the serene one, knowing that the phenomenal universe is mere illusion, and being without any curiosity regarding it, be affected by any fear even with the approach of death?" (56)

"With whom can we compare the most superior being, abiding in Consciousness, perfectly content, not desirous of anything, even liberation?" (57)

"Why should the serene one who is aware of the emptiness of all phenomenal objects have any preference for things as being acceptable or unacceptable." (58)

"He who has ceased to conceptualize and is, therefore, free from attachment to sense objects, beyond the interrelated pairs of opposites, and free from volition, accepts with equanimity whatever comes his way in the normal course." (59)

In this set of beautiful verses, Ashtavakra produces the portrait of a case where enlightenment has taken place, where a transformation has taken place from the phenomenal "me" to the Noumenal "I", where the perception has become entirely non-relational to objects—where, in short, the living and functioning of all phenomenal objects (including his own) is merely witnessed, in a totally impersonal way without any involvement, without any judging. In other words, the split-mind of relative duality has been healed into the wholeness of absolute Noumenality.

Ashtavakra, in fact, says to Janaka that this is what actually happens when there is true awakening, genuine enlightenment. See for yourself whether this has happened, he suggests.

The essential point in this test is not the test itself but the necessity for it. The essence of Truth is in the experiencing of it. As Nisargadatta Maharaj used to say, I am truth, meaning thereby that the experiencing of the Truth transformed the "me" into "I", the phenomenal object into the Noumenal subject. (There is really no"transformation" as such, more a wiping out of a false identity that was superimposed). Anyway, *Truth, when it is conceptualized and vocalized (by whoever it may be) no longer remains Truth but becomes a concept*. A similar sort of transformation must occur in a disciple, and the *guru* considers it his duty to "test" the disciple in regard to the reaction of his words (his pointers to the Truth), to find out whether there was adequate receptivity in the disciple. In testing his disciple, the *guru* is not so much concerned with his own ability to impart knowledge as with the disciple's capacity to understand and absorb that knowledge. It is really very deep compassion—*karuna*—which makes the *guru* so keen and anxious that enlightenment should occur in the case of the disciple. The *guru*, as a *jnani*, is certainly fully aware of the total implications of the occurrence of enlightenment. He knows it is an impersonal happening and that Noumenally there is no question really of anything happening even impersonally. But the fact remains that phenomenally, even conceptually, deep inherent compassion is present in every *jnani*, as it was present in the Buddha, and it is this compassion which makes the *guru* do his best for the disciple.

First, Ashtavakra asks Janaka to make sure that there is not the slightest remnant of any fear of death, no mental reservations regarding the dissolution of the body and of the ego. He wants Janaka to know absolutely that the ego does not survive the dissolution of the body, that it will not get a new body in course of time, because enlightenment can occur only when the ego, the "me"—the basis of which is duration—is completely extinguished. Then, Ashtavakra proceeds to the sense of equanimity which is constantly present in the *jnani*, and because of which he is impervious to pleasure and pain, gain or loss, praise or criticism. The *jnani* sees the working of his own body like that of any other body, and he is totally free of any volition and desire, even the desire for enlightenment. He has no preference for things "acceptable" as against things "unacceptable" because he is totally contented. He accepts what comes naturally in the course of his life without any sense of volition so that for him there is nothing to be done or not to be done. In other words, Ashtavakra gives Janaka a very tight "check-list" (one that leaves him little scope for rationalization). Janaka must find out for himself what his own spiritual level is.

When the *guru* sets such a test for the disciple, the very first reaction from the disciple (not to the contents of the test but to the fact that the test itself is being set), is most important and immediately reveals the caliber of the disciple. Janaka was wise enough and mature enough to realize that it was through compassion for him that the *guru* had set the test and not out any perverse desire to fail him. If he had shown the slightest resentment, he would have exposed his own ego so very clearly that Ashtavakra need not have waited for the answer to his test. Since he had well and truly grasped the *guru*'s teaching Janaka, on the contrary, responds with great humility and sheer gratitude that his *guru* should have found him worthy of being tested. Any other response would have created perhaps an unbridgeable separation between the *guru* and the disciple. But obviously the time was ripe, the disciple mature and ready for enlightenment, and the *guru* equally enthusiastic to supply that spark which would bring it about. Therefore, Janaka's reaction is not only quite appropriate but his response equally natural and spontaneous, and therefore more importantly, effortless and sincere. There is no hesitation in his answer, no interference from the split mind, no anxiety whether his answer comes from within and therefore it cannot help reaching his *guru*'s heart. Neither the query nor the answer has any dialectic basis; only the heart is concerned, not the mind.

Janaka addresses the *guru* (in the answer contained in six verses) with the word "*Hanta*", a short form of "*Arihanta*" or "*Ashita*", meaning one who has overcome one's enemies, namely, the six traditional affective emotions of desire, anger, envy, attachment, arrogance and jealousy—in short, the ego which is the basis of all the phenomenal trouble. Once the ego is exposed and driven out, its phenomenal manifestations cease automatically. This very form of respectful address, which came out so spontaneously, must have gratified Ashtavakra and removed all doubts, if any had lingered. Janaka's answer in the six verses following this form of address could only have strengthened Ashtavakra's conviction, pride and joy in his remarkable disciple.

Says Janaka:

"0, Hanta, the man of understanding, knowing his true nature, who takes part in the game of living, can never be compared with the beasts who carry burdens in life." (60)

Janaka clearly implies that having been enlightened by Ashtavakra's stirring words which have suddenly shown him his true nature, he no longer regards life as being full of miseries, as most people do. And yet his answer also implies several things. He does not phrase his answer—or, rather, his answer is not phrased—in personal terms. This implies that he has not now become an enlightened *individual*. He has also indicated in general terms that the enlightenment has come about suddenly, that nothing has really changed except that the personal identity, the entitification, which caused the bondage through a mistaken sense of volition and responsibility, has disappeared. In its wake there is a feeling of such freedom and joy that life and living now seems a *lila*, a game in which the interrelated opposites of pleasure and pain arise on the surface (like waves on the ocean) and soon disappear.

> *"Abiding in that state which Indra and the other gods hanker after pitifully, the yogi is not particularly elated." (61)*

The *yogi*—the *jnani*—is not particularly elated because he is established in his natural state, the Noumenal state that transcends all pain and pleasure which are phenomenal experiences. Indeed, what Janaka points out is that all the pitfalls, which Ashtavakra has so very compassionately indicated, have all been transcended. They cannot affect him anymore because he is fully aware that all phenomenal objects are mere appearances, concepts which have no nature of their own. He also brings out the fact that Indra and the other gods are only conceptual creations, and an object, (a concept), cannot be enlightened, whether he is a sentient being or a god.

> *"The heart of the jnani is not touched by virtue and vice, just as the sky is not affected by smoke even though it might appear so." (62)*

The *jnani* is not affected by the operations of the interrelated opposites like virtue and vice which are only phenomenal concepts because he is not involved with any actions which might take place through "his" psychosomatic organism. There is only witnessing. The sky of the *jnani's* witnessing is not affected by the smoke and pollution of the phenomenal actions that are taking place as part of the functioning of totality. Phenomenal actions can affect only an object through their consequences, but when the "me" has been totally demolished, the "I" forever transcends all phenomenality. In an indirect, respectful way, Janaka is assuring his *guru* with supreme confidence that the ego has indeed been annihilated.

"Who can prevent the Self-realized one, who has known the unicity of the unmanifest Noumenon and the phenomenal manifestation, from acting as he wishes?" (63)

"Acting as he wishes" clearly means spontaneous actions for the simple reason that the *jnani* has no will or volition of his own. Therefore, all actions which appear to be those of an individual are, in reality, the spontaneous activity of the Noumenal functioning. In this verse, Janaka brings out the fact that although some actions of "his" might *appear* to have the taint of not conforming to scriptural injunctions, they are not the actions of an identified individual with supposed volition. As such, they are totally impersonal without the slightest touch of doership. In other words, all activity, appearing to be performed by the *jnani*, is spontaneous Noumenal activity *of that moment*. It is merely witnessed by the *jnani*, without any involvement, without any judging. If someone has been helped, it is not because of his wish. If someone has not been helped, it is not in spite of his wish! The *jnani* lives only in the present moment, not concerned with duration.

"Of the four kinds of created beings [1], from Brahma to a blade of grass, it is only the wise one who is capable of renouncing both desire and aversion." (64)

"Rare is the man who knows the Noumenon as one without a second, the lord of the universe. He does what he considers worth doing and has no fear from any quarter." (65)

---

1 Born from a womb, born from an egg, born from vapor or sweat, born from seed.

In these two verses, Janaka talks of the "wise one" renouncing both desire and aversion, and of his doing whatever he considers worth doing without fear from any quarter. Thereby it is clear that Janaka has not withdrawn completely into that impersonality which assumes all doing and non-doing as phenomenal functioning of the Noumenon. Ashtavakra, therefore, in the next four verses reminds him that there really is no individual doer doing any renouncing, and that what ultimately happens is dissolution of the "me" into the subjective "I."

"Since you are pure, unattached beingness, where is the question of your renouncing anything? All that is necessary is the disidentification with the psychosomatic apparatus and the dissolution of the illusion of the "me" into the Noumenal "I." (66)

"In the knowledge that the universe arises in yourself as the Consciousness, like bubbles in the ocean, enter into the state of dissolution." (67)

"In the knowledge that the appearance of the phenomenal universe is an illusion, like that of the snake in the rope, and that, although it seems real to the senses, you as the pure Noumenon completely transcend it, enter into the state of dissolution." (68)

"In the knowledge that you are perfection itself, the potential fullness of plenum, the unchanged in misery and happiness, hope and despair, life and death, enter into the state of dissolution." (69)

To begin with, Ashtavakra tells Janaka that he has only to give up the identification with the body in order to be liberated. He is suggesting that the identification is the obstruction, the destruction of which will bring him liberation. There is in this suggestion a relation between cause and effect and therefore it is still in the realm of phenomenal duality. He is deliberately setting a subtle trap to find out how deeply the disciple has intuitively absorbed the core of his teaching, that there is no bondage, therefore there cannot be any emancipation and that total freedom is the very nature of the human being.

Then Ashtavakra goes on to ask Janaka to get enlightened (through dissolution) through the knowledge that the phenomenal universe has arisen in himself as the Consciousness, like bubbles on the surface of the ocean. Again, Ashtavakra makes enlightenment dependent on certain knowledge as if enlightenment would disappear if that knowledge disappeared!

Yet again, Ashtavakra tells him that the appearance of the phenomenal universe, though appearing so real, is an illusion like that of the snake in the rope, and is outside his pure beingness, and, through this knowledge, to merge in enlightenment.

Finally, Ashtavakra impresses upon Janaka the importance of equanimity in regard to the interrelated opposites like pain and pleasure, hope and despair, life and death.

In all these suggestions, there is a veiled element of "doing" something so that Janaka might "acquire" enlightenment, and Ashtavakra is anxiously waiting for Janaka's reaction to these cunning suggestions. The point is that the *guru* understands the level of the disciple's receptivity through the depth of his understanding. The *guru* wants to know whether the disciple has the keenness of intelligence to understand not only the words but the meaning and wisdom behind the apparent words.

Again, Ashtavakra must have been very pleased by Janaka's answers to his *guru*'s specific advice contained in these four verses.

Janaka says:

"I am limitless as the space whereas the phenomenal world is like a pot. This is knowledge. There is no question therefore of any renouncement or any acceptance or any dissolution." (70)

"I am like the ocean and the phenomenal universe is like a wave. This is knowledge. There is therefore no question of any renouncement or any acceptance or any dissolution." (71)

"I am like the mother-of-pearl and the illusion of the universe is like that of the silver. This is knowledge. There is therefore no question of any renouncement or any acceptance or any dissolution." (72)

"I am indeed present in all beings and all beings are in Me. This is knowledge. There is therefore no question of any renouncement, or any acceptance or any dissolution." (73)

In the earlier section, Ashtavakra had spoken of the matter of dissolution and had described the various ways in which the personal consciousness could be merged (dissolved) into the universal Consciousness. In these four verses, the worthy disciple very humbly expresses the four basic aspects of all that needs to be understood, and at the same time ventures to suggest that having apperceived the Truth, the question of "doing" anything by way of accepting or renouncing, or merging anything with something else does not really arise. One can only imagine how supremely happy the *guru* must have felt at his disciple's depth of understanding. Janaka in fact says that he has clearly understood from Ashtavakra that bondage is an illusion because he has never been anything other than totally and wholly free, the unmanifest, potential Absolute. Where then does the question arise of doing anything at all in order to "achieve" liberation? The realization is that all that exists is the limitless, formless, attributeless Noumenon within which has arisen, like waves on the ocean, the appearance of the phenomenal universe. The realization of this one fact is all the knowledge necessary to apperceive one's true nature: Noumenon is What-We-Are, the phenomenal objects are what we *appear to be.*

Janaka continues:

"In Me, the boundless ocean, the bark of the universe gets tossed about by the winds of its own inherent nature. I am not affected." (74)

"In Me, the limitless ocean, let the waves of the universe arise and then disappear according to their inherent nature. I experience neither an expansion nor a contraction." (75)

"In Me, the limitless ocean, exists the illusion of the universe. Being formless, 1 am supremely tranquil. In this do I abide." (76)

"The subjective Self is not in the object, nor is the object in the Subjective Self which is infinite and without any taint of any kind. It is free from attachment and desire and thus tranquil. In this do I abide." (77)

"Indeed What-1-Am is pure Consciousness; the world is like a magician's show. How can there be any question of rejection or acceptance for Me." (78)

These five verses are an elaboration of the Truth enunciated in the earlier four verses by Janaka. Indeed those four verses could be said to contain the whole gist of whatever any sage could say about our real nature. "This is the Truth" repeats Janaka in each of those four verses, this witnessing experience that is going on in himself. Abiding in the Truth, abiding in one's real nature, is all that is necessary. You *are* the Noumenon, the Truth. To be told to do something could be misleading; because that would imply that there is something to be "acquired" by some "one" through efforts. But the individual who is supposed to make the efforts is just not there. The supposed individual is a myth, an illusion. All there is is Noumenon within which (like a magic show) has appeared the illusion of the phenomenal universe.

Janaka makes it abundantly clear in these verses that he has clearly apperceived what Ashtavakra has been trying to get him to understand, namely, that it was not that his efforts were inadequate or that they were wrong efforts but simply that the making of efforts was itself the bondage. Effort contained the illusory desire on the part of an illusory individual to achieve an illusory goal! All that was necessary was to turn his gaze inward whereas all his effort was necessarily directed outward. Mind when turned inward ceases to conceptualize, and the ceasing of conceptualizing is tantamount to liberation because the conceptualizing itself was the creation of bondage.

The matter of thoughts arising, or the mind conceptualizing, has been one of considerable confusion and misunderstanding. If Consciousness has always been free and unfettered, why did Consciousness identify itself with each individual body and thereby cause its own limitation as personal consciousness or mind and thus unnecessarily cause all this trouble about bondage and liberation in the first place?! There are two ways of looking at the question, and both perspectives dissolve the question so that an answer becomes superfluous. If Consciousness is originally and always quite unfettered, totally free, why should it *not* limit itself and thereby engage itself in the *lila* that this life is? This deliberate act of restricting itself into an individual consciousness is part of its freedom! Also, it is only through this division into subject and object relationship that Consciousness can perceive and cognize the phenomenal universe that it has "created" within itself. One sentient being becomes the subject and perceives the other sentient beings as objects, and this is the "mechanism" for Consciousness to cognize the manifestation.

Bondage does *not* arise merely by the duality of subject and object relationship. Such duality is the necessary mechanism for the cognition of phenomenality by the universal Consciousness. The *lila* of the interrelationship between human beings—"the magic show"—which Consciousness provides within itself, causing the supposed pleasure and misery to the supposed individuals in their supposed lives, is not the result of the "mechanism" of *duality* but arises through the operation of *dualism*. Dualism is caused by the entitification of each body as *a separate* subject—overlooking the basic fact that all are objects and it is the absolute Noumenon alone who is the only subject. In other words, it is this assumption of subjectivity by a phenomenal object that is the cause of the supposed bondage, and it is merely recognizing this fact that means the supposed liberation. And this is what Janaka is saying in these verses. He has recognized that what he *appears to be* is the body-mind organism but that What-He-Is is the subjective Noumenon. Therefore there is nothing to be done for the simple reason that a mere appearance, the body-mind organism is incapable of doing anything on its own because it has no autonomous, independent existence. An organism can only "live" according to its basic nature, its *dharma*, the way it has been made and conditioned. It merely fulfills its role in the *lila*, though there may be an illusion of volition and choice.

❧

CHAPTER FOUR

✤

Ashtavakra says:

"It means bondage when the mind desires something or grieves at something, rejects or accepts anything, feels happy or angry with anything." (79)

"It means liberation when the mind does not desire or grieve, or reject or accept, or feel happy or angry." (80)

"It is bondage when the mind is attached to any sense experience. It is liberation when the mind is detached from all sense experiences." (81)

"When the "me" is present, it is bondage; when the "me" is not present, it is liberation. Having understood this, it should be easy for you to refrain from accepting or rejecting anything." (82)

Ashtavakra first gives Janaka a severe test and is then obviously gratified with the way his disciple has reacted to the test and has stood his ground firmly and confidently on his apperception of the Truth. Now in the four verses comes the appreciation and encouragement from the *guru*.

Ashtavakra repeats the fact that the bondage lies firmly on the conceptualization by the mind. He makes it clear that even being happy can be a bondage because such happiness is interrelated to the concept of unhappiness or being angry. It is totally different from the sheer, pure joy of that state when the "me" is absent and there is no conceptualizing. There is "happiness" when the self is forgotten temporarily as when your mind is engrossed in some activity, be it listening to music (devotional or otherwise) or watching competitive sports or having sex or whatever. But this kind of happiness is temporary and when such activity ceases and the "cause" of such happiness is no longer present, the happiness not only disappears but sometimes gives way to depression. Abiding in the Self, without the mind doing its usual conceptualizing, means peace and a deep joy because it is not dependent on any material cause. The very nature of the natural state is peace and joy, and material happiness is a pale reflection of this state.

Ashtavakra makes it clear that the conceptualizing is the result of the "me" wanting or not wanting something. And when the "me" is not there, there is no wanting (or not wanting) and conceptualizing ceases—and this means liberation. This clearly goes directly against the usual advice given by organized religion to "renounce." If such a religious person is asked why one should practice renunciation, the answer (whatever it may be) would be on the line that one should practice renunciation in order that one should get something or other, some time or other, somewhere or other! In other words, this renunciation is itself based on the desire of the "me" to achieve something!! What Ashtavakra implies is that the "desire", the "wanting", has to go but it has to go by itself—to fall off—spontaneously as a result of understanding, and not as a deliberate volitional positive action. And the "me", with its wants and desires, falls off by itself when the mind settles into its source (Consciousness), into a state of no-mind-ness, which is its wholeness and holiness, which is not tainted by any objective relationships. There is conflict in the split-mind relationship of one object with another object. But the source of both being the same Consciousness, there is no question of any conflict when both are in a non-objective relationship in the undivided, whole mind. The relationship between one split-mind object and another split-mind object is *samsara*; the non-objective relationship in the whole-mind is *Nirvana*. The non-objective relationship in its operation is what is known as "witnessing", being aware without choosing or judging.

Ashtavakra continues:

"Who is it that is concerned with the interrelated pairs of opposites such as duties to be performed and acts to be avoided? When do they end and for whom do they end? Enquiring thus—through indifference to the world—proceed to remain without desire and volition." (83)

"Rare indeed, my child, is that blessed person whose desire for life, enjoyment and learning have been extinguished by merely observing the ways of the world." (84)

"The man of wisdom becomes serene through the realization that this world is transient and tainted by the triple misery [2] and is therefore, without substance, contemptible and to be discarded." (85)

"Is there any stage or age when the interrelated pairs of opposites do not affect people? The one

---

2 From: a) one's own organism, b) other organisms, and c) acts of nature.

who disidentifies himself from them and is content with whatever comes to him spontaneously, in the ordinary course, attains perfection." (86)

"Who *will not attain tranquility who, seeing the diversity of opinions among the many seers, saints and yogis, becomes totally indifferent?" (87)*

"Is he not the true guru *who, having apperceived his true nature as pure Consciousness, through indifference, equanimity and through dialectical reasoning, has saved himself from the metempsychosis of* samsara?" *(88)*

"The moment you perceive the different phenomena in the universe as they truly are, that is to say, different patterns and combinations of the same five basic elements, you will at once be free from bondage and you will be able to abide in your true Self." (89)*

"Intentions are the root of *samsara. Therefore, the abandoning of intention and volition means dispassion with the world, and then you can live anywhere." (90)*

Ashtavakra never allows his disciple to stray too far from the basic truth—that the root of the whole trouble is in getting involved in the thoughts and desires that keep arising. Such thoughts are based on the duality of interdependent opposites like pleasure and pain, happiness and misery. He points out that the very nature of the mind is to produce thoughts and any kind of suppression can only make matters worse. All that can be done is to witness those thoughts and desires as they arise and not get involved in them. Such witnessing keeps you away from the identification with the body as a separate entity. The different phenomena in the universe are then seen as different combinations of the same five basic elements, each phenomenon, each sentient being, behaving according to its inherent nature and the conditioning to which it has been subjected.

Thoughts into words into actions into further thoughts—that is the vicious circle of the *samsara*. Deep understanding reveals that the functioning of the total universe is based on duality and that each phenomenon is actually "being lived" according to its inherent nature and subsequent conditioning in order to serve as the respective characters in this living-dream. This understanding translates itself in actual life as "witnessing" which provides the shield against all experiences in duality. Then, the living becomes spontaneous, natural and non-volitional—Noumenal. This is all that the concept of "enlightenment" truly means.

In other words, Ashtavakra says that with understanding dawns "dispassion." The word in Sanskrit that he uses is a beautiful word which has no adequate translation in English. He says "*Udaseen*." The word is loosely used even in India in the sense of "dispassion", as a lack of interest. The word means very much more. It means, literally, "seated in the Self", a totally different dimension from space-time duality. It is the center of the *kshana*, the Here-and-Now, the infinite intemporality from where the continuous witnessing takes place of all the movements in Consciousness. Of course, such witnessing is absolutely without any involvement by way of judging anything. All thoughts, all actions, all events are part of the functioning of totality, and there is no question of any "one" judging any part of such functioning—this is itself the understanding.

Ashtavakra finally concludes that when the being itself is centered in the here-and-now, the body-mind apparatus may live anywhere for the simple reason that the body-mind apparatus, freed from the desire and volition of the "me", becomes the vehicle of the functioning of Totality.

> "Forsake desire, which is the enemy, material
> prosperity, which leads to much mischief, and also
> the performance of good deeds with the aim of
> achieving something—which is the cause of these
> two—cultivate indifference towards everything."
> (91)

> "Regard friends, lands, wealth, houses, wives, gifts,
> and other such items of good fortune as a dream or
> juggler's show lasting but a short time." (92)

> "Know that wherever there is desire, there is samsara.
> With sincere, intense dispassion, go beyond desire,
> and thus be happy." (93)

> "It is in desire that bondage exists, and liberation is
> considered to be in the destruction of desire. Only
> through non-attachment to the phenomenal world
> does one attain the perennial joy of the realization
> of Self." (94)

> "You are the pure Consciousness. The phenomenal
> universe is inert and illusory. Ignorance as such
> too does not exist. Why, therefore, your quest for
> knowledge?" (95)

> "Kingdoms, sons, wives, bodies, and sensual
> pleasures have been lost to you birth after birth,
> even though you were attached to them." (96)

> "Enough, therefore, of prosperity, desires and good

deeds. The mind did not find any repose in the dreary wilderness of samsara." *(97)*

"For how many lives have you not done hard, painful labors of body, mind and speech? At least now, desist." (98)

Dharma, artha, kama and *moksha* are the four milestones or stages in the traditional Hindu scheme of life. At this stage, Ashtavakra omits merely *moksha* (liberation) and asks his disciple to forsake both *artha* and *kama* (wealth and desire) as also *dharma*. In other words, Ashtavakra says forsake not only evil deeds but good deeds too because the "me", as the doer, is behind both kinds of deeds.

Artha (wealth) is necessary in order to fulfill *kama* (the worldly desires). Therefore for the ordinary person, still identified with the body as a separate entity—for the illusory entity engaged in the illusory worldly activity—*artha* becomes the means to achieve *kama*. Wealth is necessary in order to fulfill worldly desires. Then, when the passions and the desires and the ambitions cool down in later life, the other two come into prominence: *dharma* (good deeds) becomes the means and *moksha* (liberation) becomes the end. Ashtavakra makes, in the circumstances, what must be considered a remarkably revolutionary pronouncement. He says even *dharma* must be forsaken. This is so because tradition accepts *moksha* as a desired end which can be attained through some means, whereas liberation can *occur* only when desire has been totally absent. It is immaterial that the desire is a "good" one. The quality of the desire is not important. What is important and necessary is the total absence of desire as such. The presence of desire presupposes the presence of a "me." No "me", an illusory non-entity, can possibly be liberated. Enlightenment or liberation or awakening or whatever is only a happening which occurs in appropriate circumstances at the appropriate time through an appropriate psychosomatic apparatus. It is not something attainable through any means or by any effort. In other words, what Ashtavakra says is that the true nature of every phenomenon, every sentient being, is the Noumenon, the absolute subjectivity. It is ridiculous for an object to seek its subjectivity. All there is is the Noumenal subjectivity of which the entire phenomenal manifestation (and every thing therein) is its objective expression.

It is extremely difficult for an ordinary man to grasp the fact that nothing more than a deep understanding of one's true nature is necessary for the transformation to take place. It has been man's conditioning from the earliest day of his life that it is only effort which could bring him anything in life. As a baby he had to cry before his hunger was satisfied. And now he is told by a *guru* like Ashtavakra or Nisargadatta Maharaj that understanding is all, and that any effort by a "me" could well be counterproductive. It seems incredible, almost unacceptable. But the fact of the matter is that an individual is merely an appearance in Consciousness, and as such cannot have any existence or entitification which can either be under bondage or be liberated therefrom. Bondage and liberation are merely concepts. As soon as these concepts are given up and conceptualization ceases, the illusory individual disappears into his source, the Self or Consciousness, along with the rest of the phenomenal manifestation.

Ashtavakra asks his disciple to clearly see the illusoriness and the *time-bound* nature of all phenomena: whatever is perceivable is perishable. Anything susceptible to change is perishable, and the very essence of phenomenality is change and movement. And, Ashtavakra assures Janaka, your true nature is that which is unperceivable, unchangeable. He therefore advises his disciple to ensure that his dispassion is not superficial but that it is sincere and intense. Then he will no longer be susceptible to desire, the existence of which means involvement in *samsara*. Dispassion or renunciation, which is based on a certain result in this world or hereafter and therefore rooted in desire, is neither intense nor sincere. It is essentially a kind of bargaining with a super-entity, a super power called God. Certain things will be given up on the understanding that certain other things (more desirable) will be made available, in the present or in the hereafter. This is not the kind of renunciation to which Ashtavakra refers. There is no need for him to go into detailed explanations for he has already realized that his disciple is not a recent initiate into spirituality. Nonetheless he repeatedly impresses upon the disciple that desire (which is based on volition) of any kind is the ultimate block to spiritual awakening. Indeed, the very desire for enlightenment is a block because the basis of any desire, however noble, is the "me" entity, and awakening cannot *occur* so long as the "me" exists. The true *guru* is interested only in the total annihilation of the "me" entity and how well Ashtavakra has succeeded will be seen by the way Janaka responds to this stirring advice.

Ashtavakra warns his disciple that desire will destroy itself gradually, but only when its power of destruction is constantly borne in mind. By this he suggests that no positive action like suppressing desire could ever achieve any success in destroying desire. On the contrary, any positive action will only strengthen desire. The only way to destroy desire is to witness passively the arising of desire each time it happens, without any involvement. Such witnessing will cut off vertically any horizontal extension of the desire which involvement clearly indicates. Even the active quest for knowledge could be considered a positive action. Ashtavakra assures Janaka that he is the pure Consciousness whereas all else is illusory, including ignorance. Wherefore, he asks, the quest for knowledge?! Why, too, the need for doing good deeds, the basis of which is again a desire for something in return? Finally, he reminds the disciple about all the positive efforts that he has put in, life after life, for the acquisition of knowledge and enlightenment. All these efforts have been an exercise in futility. At least now, he appeals to his disciple, stop all positive effort and *just be.*

In the following eight verses, Ashtavakra summarizes the basis of true understanding resulting in a certain type of conviction which fundamentally precludes any kind of question and doubt, and thus results in what might be called non-volitional action in daily life.

"In the conviction that continuous change and ultimate destruction after a certain duration is the very nature of all phenomena, the man of wisdom remains unperturbed, free from misery and relaxed in his attitude." (99)

"In the conviction that the phenomenal manifestation has no nature other than the Noumenon which is immanent in all phenomena, the man of wisdom remains contented and relaxed with all desires, completely pacified and unattached to anything whatever." (100)

"In the conviction that adversity and prosperity come in their turn as effects of past actions, as causality, the man of wisdom, contented, with his senses in passive restraint, wants nothing and grieves for nothing." (101)

"In the conviction that happiness and misery, birth and death are parts of the natural process of causality, the man of wisdom, without any need to accomplish anything, is free from anxiety and does not identify himself with anything he happens to be doing." (102)

"In the conviction that it is anxiety and nothing else

that is the root cause of misery in this world, the man of wisdom, with his desires annihilated, remains free from anxiety, happy and contented." (103)

"In the conviction J am not the body, nor is the body mine -I am pure Consciousness', the man of wisdom is indifferent to what has been achieved and what remains to be achieved, and lives in a natural state of non-volition, which is akin to the Noumenal state." (104)

"In the conviction 'I am immanent in all phenomena, from Brahma to a blade of grass', the man of wisdom is free from any conceptualizing or objectivizing, indifferent to what has been attained or not attained, and remains contented and at peace." (105)

"In the conviction that this manifested universe, wondrous though it be in the variety and diversity of its phenomena, is truly illusory, the man of wisdom, without any desires, identified with the pure Consciousness, remains in Noumenal peace." (106)

This is an extremely important set of eight verses dealing with volition, desire, and what might be called "non-volitional" living. It will have been noticed that beginning with the general principles of phenomenal manifestation and the relation of the individual with the manifestation, Ashtavakra has now arrived at the most interesting stage of how the man of wisdom (the man of understanding, the *jnani*), who has lost his identity as a separate individual, lives his life as an ordinary individual in the world.

The conviction of the man of wisdom extends over the

following aspects of understanding:

(a) continuous change leading ultimately to disintegration is the nature of all phenomena;

(b) the phenomenal manifestation has no nature other than the Noumenon which is immanent in all phenomena;

(c) adversity and prosperity are interdependent opposites which appear alternately in life and are an intrinsic part of living;

(d) happiness and misery, birth and death (and all other polaric contraries) are parts of the natural process of causality;

(e) anxiety is the root cause of misery in the world;

(f) "I am not the body, nor is the body mine—I am pure Consciousness";

(g) "I am immanent in all phenomena from *Brahma* to a blade of grass";

(h) this manifested universe, wondrous though it be in the variety and diversity of its phenomena, is truly illusory.

The result of this eight-pronged conviction is that the man of wisdom remains unperturbed, free from anxiety and misery, contented and relaxed, without any more desires, indifferent to what has been achieved or attained, unachieved or unattained, and thus remains in Noumenal peace, identified with the pure Consciousness. What all desires, achievements or their lack, attainments or their lack, happiness and misery boils down to is the matter of volition or intentions. The man of wisdom is wise to the fact that as an apparent entity he cannot live according to this own sweet will and pleasure. He is truly convinced that he is in fact *being lived*, that as such—as an apparent entity—he cannot possibly be the subject of objects. The apparent entity, a phenomenal object like all phenomenal objects, cannot have other objects as his objects. Thus knowing what he is not, the man of wisdom knows what he *truly is*: "I am pure Consciousness."

Knowing that he cannot live according to his will or volition, that he is in fact "being lived" (as an instrument of the Totality), he also knows the futility of "intentions." By abstaining from volition the man of wisdom is free of anxiety and misery, because then he transcends conceptualization which is the basis of volition and intention. Knowing that he is being lived, the man of wisdom transcends both volitional action and its counterpart, volitional non-action: volitional non-doing is also doing. It is for this reason that the man of wisdom goes about his business in the ordinary way without any intentions, without any sense of doership.

It is only the "me"-concept that can have intentions because "will" and "ego" are synonymous terms. Thus the absence of volition in the case of the man of wisdom does not mean phenomenal inaction but the absence of volitional action (positive or negative). The absence of volitional phenomenal action can only mean the presence of Noumenal action. In other words, the nonvolitional action of the man of wisdom (whether perceptive, conceptive, or somatic) is Noumenal action, the non-action of the sage (because the "me" and his intention is totally absent).

Enlightenment is the *inevitable* result of the absence of purposeful intentions. The absence of purposeful intentions means the absence of conceptualization. But thoughts as such are totally spontaneous and involuntary. The absence of conceptualizing or objectivizing by the man of wisdom means he does not judge other objects and their actions. The objectivizing of the sage or man of wisdom thus means perceiving objects as objects but not as *"his" objects*. He knows with the deepest of conviction that neither "he" nor the "others" are separate independent entities but that all are merely puppets reacting to external stimuli according to psychic conditions which are beyond their control.

Non-volitional living (implying, of course, absence of both aspects of volition)—being lived as a non-entity—is subjective or Noumenal living in which, in the absence of the phenomenal "me", there is no room for anxiety or worry. It is for this reason that often the very first overpowering effect of the happening known as awakening or reintegration is a sense of incredible, total freedom.

CHAPTER FIVE

❧

Janaka now responds to Ashtavakra's instruction contained in the previous verses. The dialogue now reaches considerable heights of spiritual elegance and subtlety. He has listened to the brief but vivid description of the understanding of the man of wisdom given by Ashtavakra, and now proceeds to narrate his own current state of mind, leaving it to the *guru* to judge it and guide him further.

Janaka says:

"I became indifferent to and detached from first physical action, then small talk and finally conceptualizing itself, and so I abide in my natural state." (107)

"Without any attachment to words and sense objects, and as the Self is not an object of perception, my mind has been freed from distraction and become one-pointed. And so do I abide in my natural state." (108)

"Having realized that efforts such as meditation are prescribed only for those whose mind is distracted,

I abide in my natural state." (109)

"0 Brahman, I have seen through the unreality of the interrelated opposites like pleasure and pain, the acceptable and the unacceptable, and so I abide in my natural state." (110)

"Having found that limiting myself to the duties of the particular life stage and observing the prescribed self-disciplines, etc. are distractions, I abide in my natural state." (111)

"Having fully realized that deliberately abstaining from action is as much the outcome of ignorance as the volitional action, I abide. (112)

"Thinking on the Unthinkable means another aspect of conceptualizing and objectivizing. Having realized this, I abide in my natural state." (113)

"Blessed is the man who has accomplished this. Blessed is he, indeed, whose very nature is this." (114)

Janaka describes in these verses the gradual transformation that has taken place in the course of the annihilation of what he had been conditioned to believe was his identity. Gone is the identification with the phenomenal object, the psychosomatic apparatus, totally devoid of any substance or autonomy that was merely an appearance in Consciousness, and not an entity at all. Indeed, he has come to realize that all the hard work the "seekers" put in by following the prescribed techniques and methods are all to no purpose because they continue to cling to the illusion that they themselves are entities with independence to work and achieve something. He has clearly understood that whatever the seekers attempt to do will amount to naught, so long as they consider "themselves" as "doing" it as independent and autonomous entities, no matter how "holy" and unselfish the doing or the not-doing may be. This is so because while they may have seen the illusory nature of the universe and everything in it, they have not yet realized that, as an intrinsic part of the phenomenal universe, they themselves are also illusory! The individual do-er is illusory, therefore the doing must necessarily also be in duration and therefore illusory.

In other words, Janaka tells his *guru* that having apperceived the illusory nature of what he himself *appears* to be in the phenomenal manifestation, he abides in his natural state. This, of course, is the Noumenal state from which has arisen the entire manifestation as a dreamed appearance in Consciousness. He makes it abundantly clear that he has had the direct intuitive apperception of the truth that he is the inconceivable infinity. The bodymind phenomenon (with which he had identified himself through ignorance) is merely an appearance in Consciousness, an insubstantial shadow.

To begin with, Janaka says he has realized that the working of the body (the respiratory, the digestive, the nervous, and other systems) is almost entirely on its own, needing no conscious direction for its functioning. He has also realized that the stream of thoughts flows by itself if there is no involvement. Thus no personal involvement is at all necessary.

This dialogue between Ashtavakra as the *guru* and Janaka as the superior disciple is not in the nature of a debate between individuals but a sort of union between Consciousness and Consciousness, a sort of sharing the state of fulfillment.

Without attachment to sound (word), says Janaka, he has

realized that words with their meanings and implications are all movements in Consciousness, mental modifications which have no repercussions on the Self. Therefore, he has transcended the usual psychic reactions to words. Words are merely sounds and when seen in this light, there is no need to react to anything that is said. And when this is realized, there is no need to flee from society into a forest and become a recluse. Indeed, such a course—escaping from society—is a negative approach with consequences totally opposite to what is expected. The dangers with which living in society are supposed to confront a seeker are truly a challenge to his understanding. Until there is the conviction in the seeker that all phenomena are merely appearances without any substance, there can be no true understanding as such. And when the seeker begins to see all objects as objects without assuming the subjectivity of the Noumenon, then there is no subject-object conflict. This non-objective relationship is true perceiving leading to awakening.

Janaka then proceeds to the matter of meditation. He says that he finds no need for any action including meditation because that would presuppose the acquisition of something, even if though it be the holy object of achieving liberation. He makes the bold statement that he finds all such methods and efforts to be distractions and that instead he simply abides in his natural state. When he abides in that natural state, all interdependent opposites negate each other and disappear completely and there is nothing to be accepted or rejected. Even thinking about the unthinkable is an exercise in futility. All that is necessary, says Janaka, is to abide in one's real nature.

Janaka concludes this set of eight verses by exclaiming how truly simple it is to give up all effort and thereby negate the conceptual do-er who is the villain. And then there is nothing to attain, nothing to achieve. One is home!

Janaka continues:

"The tranquility that is the result of the conviction that the entire manifestation is a phenomenal illusion is rare even for ones who possess only a loin-cloth. Therefore, giving up the very concept of renunciation and acceptance, I remain contented in my natural state." (115)

"There is weariness of the body here, the fatigue of the tongue there and distress of the mind elsewhere. Therefore, detached from all action and effort, I remain happily in my natural state." (116)

"Clearly understanding that nothing is actually "done" in Reality, I remain established in my natural state witnessing whatever happens to be done." (117)

"The spiritual seekers are involved in action or inaction because they are still identified with the body. Not being concerned with either identity or non-identity, I live happily in my natural state." (118)

"No consequences—good or evil—concern me whether in movement or at rest. Therefore, I am content in my natural state whether the body-mind apparatus is stationary, in movement or asleep." (119)

"I do not lose anything by relaxing, nor do I gain anything by striving. Therefore, transcending all concepts of loss or gain, I remain happily in my natural state." (120)

"Having repeatedly observed the inconstancy of the various aspects of pleasure in varying circumstances, lam indifferent to all experience and remain happily in my natural state." (121)

What Janaka says clearly in these seven verses is that he has faced the facts squarely and has come to the inevitable conviction that the entire manifestation is a phenomenal illusion. This conviction has given him a sense of contentment and peace which even the renunciate with only a loin-cloth probably does not feel. This conviction comports the faith that there cannot be a path for any "one" to go any "where"; nor can there be anything to "do" -because there just is not any autonomous or independent entity to go anywhere or do anything.

So, what is the conclusion? Obviously, not to conceive any thinking, speaking or doing as being due to our illusory volition, since every phenomenal action and experience of every sentient being is an expression of our Noumenality If effort is needed at all, it is certainly not in order to see the simple truth the Masters have given us since time immemorial. The truth is that all that we could be must inevitably be Noumenal, and that what we *appear* to be cannot be anything but phenomenal and therefore illusory. If effort is needed at all, it could only be to eradicate the conditioning (generally called "ego") which makes people do what they *feel* is right for *them* to do. It is not easy to overcome conditioned or reflex action.

In spite of all the teaching by the Masters. People will continue to practice all kinds of self-torture even though they cause "weariness to the body", "fatigue to the tongue" and "distress to the mind", without realizing that such self-discipline and even consecration could well mean reinforcing the ego which prevents them from "remaining happily in my natural state."

Janaka's understanding of the illusoriness of the

phenomenal manifestation and its functioning as a living dream in Consciousness includes the inherent realization that the supposed volition of the individual cannot alter the inexorable functioning of the totality. What must happen will inevitably happen. Therefore, says Janaka, he is content merely to witness whatever happens in life. There is a Sufi story which is rather pertinent to this point. There was a small but very prosperous kingdom in which all were prosperous in their various respective fields of activity, except one astonishingly unlucky person who failed in whatever activity he engaged himself. He was a very nice person in every way, always willing to extend his help to anyone who needed it, and everyone felt very sorry for him. One day, the elders went to the king and suggested that something should be done for him. The king, a very wise man, told them that he seemed to be naturally very unlucky and that nothing could really be done for him, but that he would be willing to try an experiment. So, they decided to place a pot full of gold coins in the middle of a small, narrow bridge which the unfortunate man had to cross every evening on his way home. All traffic was stopped on the bridge that evening, and the king and his associates waited on the other side. The man came along in his usual shuffling, rambling way, and stopped at the top of the bridge. Suddenly, he closed his eyes and went very slowly along one wall of the bridge until he reached the other end, his eyes still closed. The pot of gold coins was, of course, still lying in the middle of the bridge, untouched. The people waiting for him at the end of the bridge got hold of him and asked him why he had suddenly closed his eyes when he started to cross the bridge. The man shamefacedly told them that he had very often thought of some day crossing that bridge with his eyes closed, and this day when he found the bridge deserted, he could not resist the temptation!

So, says Janaka, I take things as they come believing neither in action nor in inaction, neither in profit nor loss, neither happiness nor misery, and thus I reside contentedly in my natural state.

Janaka continues:

"He whose worldly recollections have been extinguished, who is in reality, naturally vacant-minded, whose senses respond to their objects without any apparent volition, goes through life as if he were asleep." (122)

"When once my desires have melted away, where is the question of any riches, or friends, or thieves in the form of sense-objects? Where, indeed is the question of scriptures, and even knowledge?" (123)

"As I have realized my identity with the supreme absolute, the witness, there is complete indifference both to bondage and liberation, and I feel no concern even for enlightenment." (124)

"The extraordinary condition of one who is devoid of all possible doubts, and goes about as if unaware of his surroundings, uninhibitedly, can be understood only by those who are like him." (125)

This is Janaka's concluding effort to put into words the condition of the man of wisdom (the *jnani*) as he goes about his business in daily life.

Janaka refers to the man of wisdom as one "whose worldly recollections have been extinguished, who is *naturally* vacant-minded." This implies that the man of wisdom has ceased to conceptualize and objectivize because he has seen through the illusory nature of the "me", the split-mind who does the conceptualizing. The vacant mind of the man of wisdom is the result of this cessation of objectivization which itself is the result of his realizing his true nature. Such a vacant mind is not the mind of an idiot but the most alert mind. It is not clouded by the sorts of images created by objectivizing. The immediate effect of objectivizing by any sentient being is to make that object (itself) appear as a "self", an autonomous entity responsible for all its apparent actions. Coincidentally a similar autonomy will be imposed on every other phenomenal entity thus objectivized. The point is that such assumed responsibility is wholly illusory. It produces the functional aspect of the "ego" through the assumed volition, resulting in experiences of conflict, disharmony, suffering etc., also known as bondage. The deep understanding of this fact brings about in the man of wisdom the annihilation of identification (with an objective image in mind) and the conceptual bondage associated with it.

All desire is based on the "me", the identification with an objective image in the mind, and when this identification has been annihilated, all desires also vanish. Therefore, asks Janaka, when all my desires have vanished, where is the question of riches, friends, and sense-objects, of scripture or even of knowledge?

The way Janaka strings along the various items which can have no further interest for him is interesting. The point he is making is that all these items are interrelated and based on "desire." Desire for wealth may wane but in its place could arise desire for fame or desire for social work or desire even for enlightenment. Whatever the aim, however honorable or holy, the desire remains desire, be it to one thing or another. But when desire itself has been eliminated, when the whole manifestation and its functioning is seen as merely an appearance, the outward flow of the mind, the objectivizing, and the search for sensual pleasures all disappear. The mind becomes vacant. Then the phenomenal universe, instead of being perceived "without', is apperceived "within" so that it becomes "the kingdom of Heaven."

This is the state Janaka describes when conceptualization has ceased. There is complete indifference both to bondage and liberation. He feels no concern even for enlightenment. He has apperceived that the entire universe is an appearance in Consciousness, that this Consciousness, in which we all mutually appear, is perceived and cognized objectively by us as the phenomenal universe. It is precisely What-We-Are. The significant point is that we are neither different nor separate from Consciousness and for that very reason we cannot "apprehend" it. Nor can we be integrated in it because we have never been separated from it. What is important is the apprehension as such that Consciousness is not an object, and therefore we can never understand it so long as we continue to think in relative terms. And what is even more important is to apperceive that *there is nothing to be "done."* There is no need to try to understand what we are through descriptions or examples or illustrations that could only be objectivizations. Does light need to know that it is light? If there were only one man in the world, would he need to know that he was a man? All is Consciousness and we are That. To the question "How will I know when I am enlightened?" the only answer could be, "The question will not arise because you will then not need to know!"

Finally, Janaka concludes this quartet of verses with the pronouncement that the condition of enlightenment can be understood only by someone within whom a similar condition has also occurred. When the identity as a separate phenomenal entity has been demolished, the particular psychosomatic apparatus is no longer subject to the illusory notion of individual volition. "He" becomes the instrument through which the Totality functions, and therefore all "his" actions become totally spontaneous. If such a "person" were to be asked what "he" would do in a given set of circumstances, the only answer would be, "I do not know."

❧

CHAPTER SIX

✥

Having listened to the spontaneous utterances of Janaka, the *guru* Ashtavakra is pleased with the transformation that has clearly taken place, the metanoesis (the *para-vritti*) that has occurred. This sense of gratification brings about a response from the *guru* which is at once spontaneous and encouraging for the disciple. The state that is common in the case of both the *guru* and the disciple—which is itself a conceptual event in phenomenality—arises because there is in the disciple a total dis-identification with a separate entity. And there then takes place an embrace between the *guru* and the disciple in the form of a spontaneous exchange or outburst of words describing that state which is truly indescribable.

When such an exchange of dialogue between the *guru* and the Self-realized disciple (a spontaneous outpouring), is viewed purely from the intellectual point of view, it would be seen as unnecessary repetition. But from the viewpoint of a sincere seeker, it would bring tears of joy as would a piece of classical music expertly rendered by a musical maestro, however often the aficionado might have heard it before. To the music lover each rendering brings out something unique, something he had never felt before. There is no need to compare and judge. If you sit on the shore of the ocean and watch the waves keep rolling in, you can keep on watching the sight, and then you will realize that while they are all waves, each has some distinct personality, that in the *Unicity* there is a beautiful diversity in phenomenality which is most wondrous to behold.

Ashtavakra said:

"The person with a keen intellect becomes enlightened even when the instruction is imparted casually, whereas without it the immature seeker continues to remain confused even after a life-time of seeking." (126)

This is one the most significant verses in the entire work, and yet it has been misinterpreted hideously.

In one interpretation, it has been said, "Self-knowledge instantaneously dawns upon one who has completely purified his intellect by undergoing the necessary disciplines and endowing himself with the four qualifications required—the four qualifications being:

(1) renunciation i.e. unattachment to the pleasure and pain derived worldly objects and even to the joyful life in heaven, which is also impermanent;

(2) discrimination between the real and the unreal,

(3) acquisition of the six cardinal virtues, (a) *shama*, restraining the outgoing propensities of the mind, (b) *dama*, restraining the external sense organs through which the mind attaches itself to sense-objects, (c) *uparati* , withdrawing the self, (d) titiksha, forbearance, (e) *samadhana* selfsettledness, (f) *shraddha*, faith—the faith that is the grasp upon the ultimate, the faith in the power of one's own self;

(4) *samadhi*, profound meditation."

Such interpretation leaves the impression that it is up to the individual to make conscious efforts to build up a kind of intellect, to "purify" the intellect to be able to achieve some *thing* called enlightenment. Indeed what Ashtavakra says is almost the opposite. He says that a seeker could spend a lifetime of seeking trying to acquire something to enable him to acquire another thing called enlightenment, and yet remain as confused as ever. He says the desire to acquire something (even if it is some "object" called enlightenment) is itself the obstruction, and that to understand this apparently simple fact needs a keen or "pure" intellect. It needs a kind of simplicity of intellect which can accept this letting-go of wanting anything, even enlightenment! Such simplicity or purity or maturity of intellect leaves the intellect open or "vacant" to receive the apperception that all there is is Consciousness, and that therefore there cannot be anything other than that to be achieved by any conceptual individual.

It is this very fact which is emphasized by the dictum

"Na ayam atma bala-heenena labhyah", which means "Self realization is not available to those who are `weak'". And, of course, predictably, the word "weak" has been interpreted as without the strength and determination to undergo a lot of disciplines and hard work. Therefore seekers undergo a lifetime of seeking and still remain confused. What "weakness" truly means is a lack of courage to give up those traditional routines which were prescribed for when one was a spiritual beginner. It is the lack of courage to accept the intuitive promptings of the basic, fundamental Truth in its totality that all there is, is Consciousness.

The meaningful words in this pregnant verse are the "keen (*satvic*) intellect" which is capable of accepting enlightenment (*kritartha*). So, the meaningful questions are:

a) What is the *"satvic"* intellect?

b) What is the significance of the word *"kritartha"* which is used to indicate enlightenment?

The *satvic* intellect means essentially an intellect which is not mediocre, not immature, an intellect which has not divorced itself from intuition, not bound itself in logic and reason to the extent of keeping out all receptivity to natural, spontaneous arising of divinity. The *satvic* intellect essentially contains an inherent understanding—at least a basic feeling—that the human being is an intimate part of the totality of manifestation, and that therefore the human being cannot separate itself from nature and think in terms of any separate action and achievement, apart from the functioning of Totality.

Such *satvic* intellect alone is capable of being bold enough to have faith not in the prescriptions and prohibitions of infructuous traditional routine, but faith in the universal Truth that all there is, is Consciousness; and that all knowledge is in reality a collection of thoughts which are merely impermanent movements in Consciousness like waves on the surface of the ocean.

The word *"kritartha"*, which is used in this verse in the sense that it is only a person with the *satvic* intellect who becomes *kritartha* (enlightened or awakened or fulfilled), is an extremely significant word. The translation of the word means a combination of two words "understanding" and "action." It refers to the kind of understanding which is not merely at the intellectual level (which still leaves the question, "I have understood, but now how do I act?") but at the level where understanding transforms itself spontaneously into correct appropriate action. Such intuitive apprehension is of a totally different dimension from the ordinary intellectual comprehension. Such intuitive apprehension, which may be called "apperception", means a sudden transformation, a metanoesis. It brings about a sudden change in perspective in viewing the totality of manifestation and its functioning as life and living. Indeed, such apperception means not only freedom from ignorance or bondage, but freedom also from knowledge and the concept of enlightenment.

When the man of inferior intellect feels that he has "acquired" certain knowledge with a great deal of intellectual effort and *sadhana*, he is so proud of that knowledge that he can hardly wait to exhibit it at every possible opportunity It is only after some time that he finds out that that knowledge has not dissolved all doubt, but that on the contrary, it has raised a host of new questions and doubts.

Where the intellect is immature, and the individual keeps seeking (and wanting) enlightenment as an object for himself or herself, the wanting and the seeking continues to be the bondage. The knowledge that is sought itself becomes the bondage because such knowledge is not true understanding (without any individual comprehender) but an experience enjoyed by the seeker as an individual. Such experiences are often misconceived and misunderstood as enlightenment. It is not realized that it is only the individual object that can experience anything and that therefore, enlightenment cannot happen so long as there exists the individual wanting to experience enlightenment. And it is this kind of spiritual seeking which lands the individual in the confusion of an organized religion. The tenets, the concepts and the do's and don'ts of organized religions are in constant conflict not only with one another within itself (which leads to the necessity of "interpretation" of the written word) but also with those of other organized religions.

Ashtavakra continues:

"Absence of attachment to sense-objects is liberation; passion for sense-objects is bondage. Understand this fact, and then do as you please." (127)

"Apperception of this Truth seems to render an eloquent, wise and active person mute, dull and inactive. Knowledge of Truth does not therefore appear attractive to those who still want to enjoy

the pleasures of this world." (128)

This pair of verses is often taken as an injunction, whereas when taken together they constitute a mere statement of the fact of evolution. This is because of the words "do as you please." That the individual human being does not truly have any volition or choice of decision and action, will not be generally accepted, until it is so learnt through experience. Indeed, even this fact is a part of the evolution. Lord Krishna uses the same words "do as you please" when he tells Arjuna in the concluding chapter of the *Bhagavad Gita*, "I have thus declared to you the Truth, the deepest of all secrets; meditate on it, and then do as you please." What it really means is that the declaration of the Truth has happened as part of the functioning of Totality. The reaction to it by each of those who listen to it will also be a part of the functioning of the Totality. In many cases, the listener will not be interested in the Truth, especially if it is likely to make him lose all interest in life and living! In some cases, it will be taken as a challenge and these seekers will undertake to control their senses through various disciplines. They are destined to lead a life of confusion and frustration. But in a few cases, where the intellect is satvic and mature, the real meaning of the words will be deeply understood, and the understanding itself will be transformed into correct action without any sense of individual doership. It is all a matter of evolution in the impersonal functioning of the totality of manifestation. And this very understanding will bring about a letting-go, a smooth "going with the flow", a sense of tremendous freedom—enlightenment.

The various reactions to the same statement of Truth are themselves the spiritual evolution constantly happening in the impersonal functioning of Totality. Individual human beings are merely the instruments through which this evolution is taking place. This evolution begins with Consciousness identifying itself with each individual being as a separate entity. The identification continues through several lives, seeking pleasure through sense objects. Then suddenly in a particular body-mind organism appears the sense of dispassion for sense-objects, and the process of dis-identification, the seeking, begins and continues through several lives. Finally the process ends in a total disidentification with a body-mind organism as a separate entity. Enlightenment happens as an impersonal event in Consciousness through the instrument of a particular body-mind organism which has been conceived and created as one evolved highly enough to be able to receive the sudden apperception. It is necessary to understand two important aspects of this spiritual evolution:

(a) the evolution is an impersonal process in the functioning of Totality, and, therefore,

(b) no individual entity can be concerned as a separate doer in order to achieve enlightenment.

Sudden enlightenment does produce a certain change in outlook and perspective for the "individual" body-mind organism, particularly in the interim period between what a Taoist sage terms as "enlightenment" and "deliverance." Even after enlightenment happens, the individual must necessarily continue to function as a separate body-mind organism during the remainder of its span of life. There can, of course, be no hard and fast rule concerning the changes that will be brought about by the fact of enlightenment having happened. By and large, the individual concerned will continue to live as he did before, but it is not at all unlikely that his zest for pleasure will undergo a subtle change. He may be found to be not such "good company" as he was before. He may be found to enjoy his solitude more. Such changes are bound to take place because while the identity with the individual body must necessarily continue for the body to function in life, what is absent is the sense of doership, the sense of a separate entity. In other words, while the individual continues to live his life more or less as before, there is no longer any personal involvement in anything that happens. Whatever happens may have an immediate reaction, but it is very much on the surface, like a gentle wave on the surface of a lake. Whatever happens is merely witnessed, without any feeling of personal involvement.

In his classic work *Amritanubhava*[3], Saint Jnaneshwar describes this state as follows:

"Senses according to their nature may run towards objects which satisfy them but almost simultaneously there is the realization that the experience is not different from what he (the Self-realized person) himself is -just as when the sight meets the mirror, almost simultaneously there is the realization that the image therein is not different from the face."

The state of the Self-realized person is further described by the sage, Jnaneshwar, very graphically as under:

"In that state of the jnani, the volitional attitude is only an apparent one—all actions actually take place spontaneously."

"The place of duality is gradually taken over by non-duality and the objective relationship gives way to non-objective relationship."

"In the Process of the normal working of the senses the subject/object relationship does not exist."

To those seekers who seek enlightenment not out of dispassion towards sense objects but as an object that will yield them pleasure and happiness infinitely greater than what sense objects have so far given them, the

3 See *Experience Of Immortality* by Ramesh Balsekar (Chetana, Bombay, 1984) Chapter 9

transformation enlightenment actually brings about (which they see as a sort of listlessness) seems to them confusing and discouraging. The dispassion which is at the root of a true spiritual seeking is neither the dulling of the senses through an excess of sensual enjoyment nor the suppression of senses through forced disciplines. Both these lead to frustration. It is only *after* the senses have experienced their respective objects and a sense of dispassion has arisen through a deep conviction that life and living must have a meaning that is deeper than merely enjoying the pleasure of the senses, that the genuine seeking begins.

A person who is still in the process of "enjoying life" sees another person suddenly become disinterested in life and his former friends and his old way of life because of his deep, intense interest in spirituality, and he becomes afraid of this spiritual knowledge which can bring about such a drastic transformation in a man. The knowledge of Truth comes about when dispassion arises in a man after he has learnt from personal experience that whatever life provides is very hollow (however attractive it might have seemed at the time). The man of the world becomes the man of wisdom through experiencing that non-attachment means liberation whereas passion for sense-objects is bondage. Bondage means being attached to something from which you cannot be free. Sense objects cannot bind a person who can treat them with indifference (not with timidity). Dispassion does not mean staying away from sense-objects out of a fear of attachment. That is suppression which is bound to erupt in a virulent form at some time or the other. True dispassion or detachment from something *comes about* only when there is a conviction born out of actual experience that enjoyment obtained out of sense-objects brings about ultimate frustration and a lack of fulfillment.

The point that Ashtavakra makes is that to try to become a *yogi* merely because of being impressed by the looks and deeds of a *yogi* will not succeed. It is only when a bhogi (one who enjoys sense-objects) is convinced of the hollowness of it all that he becomes ready to become a *yogi*. Ashtavakra implies first a *bhogi* and then a *yogi*. Until the *bhogi* is ready to be a *yogi* he will be afraid of the knowledge, especially if he has seen a friend violently transformed from one who had a zest and lust for life into someone who is no longer interested in the good things of life. It is only after personal experience yields a deep conviction that the mind is ready to turn inward to its true nature.

To such a genuine seeker, Ashtavakra gives the direct Truth in a remarkably succinct manner as under:

"You are not the body, nor does the body belong to you. You are neither the doer nor the experiencer. You are Consciousness itself, the eternal, impersonal witness. Live happily." (129)

"Passion and aversion are attributes of the mind and you are not the mind. You are Consciousness itself, free of all conflict, changeless. Live happily." (130)

"Realizing the Self in all and all in the Self, free from the sense of 'me' and 'mine', be happy." (131)

"0, you pure Consciousness, you are indeed That in which the phenomenal universe arises like waves on the ocean. Be free from the affliction of the mind." (132)

These four verses truly constitute the very core of *Advaita*, the basis of non-duality. It seems a shame to add anything by way of comments to this set of four verses, but it is necessary to add a word or two of explanation in answer to a legitimate query: If Consciousness is all there is, and there is no individual as such, to whom is the sage addressing this instruction?

It is necessary to understand unequivocally that the sage is not really addressing this to anybody. Indeed, it is not really any instruction at all. All that the sage is doing is merely pointing to the Reality. This pointing is merely a movement in Consciousness, a part of the functioning of the Totality. It is part of the process of dis-identification in the spiritual evolution in phenomenality. Consciousness has identified itself with the individual human organism in order to create separate egos so that this life and living with the subject/object relationships may take place as *lila* (the divine play in phenomenality). Indeed, Consciousness first identifying itself with each individual as separate entity and then dis-identifying itself and recovering its impersonality is itself the *lila*. Consciousness writes the script, Consciousness produces and directs the play, Consciousness plays every role (like a one-man show) in the play, and finally Consciousness itself witnesses the play When this situation is apperceived, no doubt of any kind remains, and all there is, is Silence. Consciousness is in its primal state of absolute rest.

In some very rare cases, all this is intuitively grasped, and there is sudden awakening. But in most cases, the identification is too strong, and the evolutionary process (in phenomenality) of dis-identification is long and arduous, covering many lives.

Ashtavakra is fully aware of this fact and therefore urges the seeker to *have faith*.

He says:

"Have faith, my son, have faith. Let there be no confusion or delusion about this. You are Knowledge itself, you are the Lord, you are Consciousness, prior to all manifestation." (133)

It is necessary to understand that when the sage makes the impassioned plea "Have faith, my son, have faith", he is not thinking of "faith" as trust in someone's skill or faith in authority or faith in unverified but verifiable propositions. Ashtavakra's faith is not even the kind of faith organized religion demands in the existence and power of some supernatural entity. Nor is it faith in any form of worship that falls short of self-naughting. Ashtavakra asks for faith in the "ultimate ground", the What-Is, Consciousness which in its primal state is unaware of its own existence.

Ashtavakra then proceeds to explain that the faith he expects from the seeker is not the blind faith which some organized religions demand from their followers. He wants the seeker to look at the human being objectively and in perspective.

He says:

"The body is composed of the five elements; it comes into existence, stays for a while and then departs. The Self neither comes nor goes. Where is the sense in mourning the loss of the body?" (134)

"Whether the body lasts till the end of an eon, or it goes this moment, what difference could it make to you who are pure Consciousness?" (135)

"In you who are the infinite ocean, let the waves of phenomena appear and disappear according to their nature. It can mean no gain or loss to you." (136)

"0 my son! You are the very Consciousness within which arises this phenomenal universe that is not separate from what you are. How can there be a question of anything being acceptable or unacceptable?" (137)

"For you who are the one immutable, serene, taintless, pure Consciousness, how can there be any question o f birth or action, or even the concept of the ego?" (138)

In this series of five verses, the sage impresses upon the disciple his true nature. In essence, what he says is that all there is, is Consciousness, and that this phenomenal universe is merely an appearance which has spontaneously arisen within this Consciousness, and that, therefore, the very idea of an individual human being as a separate entity is absurd. Even so, the conditioning of an individual entity is so strong that spiritual seeking cannot *but* begin with the individual, although the seeking cannot end except with the annihilation of the individual. Therefore, the sage addresses himself hereafter to the individual from this point of view.

CHAPTER SEVEN

※

Ashtavakra says:

"Whatever you perceive is your own reflection. Can the different ornaments like bangles, amulets or anklets exist otherwise than as gold?" (139)

"Give up all distinction such as 'I am this' and 'I am not this'. Have the conviction that all there is, is Consciousness. Free from all concepts, be happy." (140)

"It is only through ignorance that the universe appears to exist. Other than you as Consciousness or Reality, nothing exists. Other than you, there is neither any individual self nor any transcendental self." (141)

"One who understands with conviction that the universe is nothing but an illusion, becomes free from desire. With the conviction that nothing exists other than Consciousness, there arises peace and serenity." (142)

"Be convinced that this apparent ocean of the manifested universe is in reality nothing but Consciousness. You are truly not concerned either with bondage or with liberation. Live freely and happily." (143)

"O, pure Consciousness that you are! Do not concern yourself with concepts of affirmations and negations. Abide in the silence of the eternal bliss that you are, and live happily." (144)

"Give up conceptualizing altogether. Have no beliefs or concepts of any kind. You are the ever free Consciousness. How can any thinking help you in any way?" (145)

What a tremendous impassioned plea the sage makes to the illusory individual! Actually, the sage is fully aware that this dialogue is in fact between the universal, impersonal Consciousness and the identified, personal consciousness, part of the process in phenomenal duration of the spiritual evolution. Nonetheless he plays the role of the teacher to perfection. He knows that this is *lila*, the functioning of the Totality of manifestation, the dream-play that is scripted by Consciousness, produced and directed by Consciousness, with every character therein being played by Consciousness.

This is precisely what the sage has in mind when he says, "Whatever you perceive is your own reflection." The observer is the observed. Who is the perceiver? Consciousness is the perceiver. The body is merely the mechanism through which the perceiving takes place. In the absence of consciousness, the body (which is merely a collection of materials) cannot do any perceiving. The individual perceiver (as the ego considers itself) is as much of an object as the perceived. Both are objective expressions of the subjective Consciousness. It is in this perspective that the sage tells the disciple that whatever he (as the misconceived individual perceiver) perceives is "your own reflection." Both are objects and the true perceiver is Consciousness. Strictly speaking, there is neither the perceiver nor the perceived; there is only perceive-*ing* as the subjective functioning. The observer object and the observed object are merely the two ends of the process of perceiving.

This aspect of the teaching of *Advaita*—that the observer is the observed, that all objects in the totality of manifestation are the expressions of the one subjective Reality—is the very basis of the teaching, and the most difficult for the mind-intellect to accept. It has been my experience that the illustration which follows has been effective in many cases: suppose you were to have ten photographs taken in ten different costumes, each with an appropriate facial make-up. The uninformed observer will naturally believe that they are photos of ten different persons. But you know that in all of them the real person is only yourself. All that has happened in this living world is that Consciousness has created the billions and billions of objects (as its own representations) which constitute the totality of manifestation. Consciousness has infused some of these objects (animals and human beings) with an aspect of itself called "sentience." This gives them a sense of individual presence, whereby they consider themselves as separate individuals, as entities separate from the others. In reality all are three-dimensional representations of Itself in different shapes and sizes, each with different inherent characteristics, in infinite variety.

In a lovely poetic image the sage Jnaneshwar says that it is *Shakti* (Consciousness-in-movement, or activated primal energy) who gave *Shiva* (the unmanifest, formless, Consciousness-at-rest) his very existence and status, the form and name (*nama-rupa*) through the manifestation of the universe. It was as if *Shakti* felt ashamed that her husband, in spite of all his awesome potentiality, should be formless and nameless, and so decided that he needed ornamentation (in the infinite variety of the manifestation). He also points out that the manifestation, the appearance, like the reflection of an object in the mirror, provides proof not of the existence of two objects but only of the original object. *Unicity* provides the illusion of duality in order to prove its own existence.

There is another aspect to this matter of the perceived being your own reflection. It is a practical aspect seen in everyday life. Take the case of the confirmed grouch who, on being greeted "Good Morning" on a lovely day, responds by asking "What's good about it?" What you see depends upon your mood, and that your moods are themselves a reflection of your deeper understanding. Someone who has been conditioned to be unusually cautious and suspicious, will naturally regard everyone he meets as an enemy. What he perceives will be tinted by his conditioning. When such conditioning exists, it will be not only futile but actually frustrating to be asked to "love thy neighbor." Love for the neighbor can arise only when there is an understanding deep enough to penetrate the earlier conditioning. The understanding is that all human beings are creations of the same Consciousness, objective expressions of the same subjective Reality. Each is conceived and created with certain given characteristics so that Consciousness in its functioning as Totality can bring about actions based on these given characteristics through the concerned organisms.

Such an understanding means an acceptance of the fact that all human beings are merely instruments through which Totality functions. In other words, when the "me" as a separate entity disappears, how can the "others" remain? Whether there is one zero or a billion zero's, what exists is only a zero unless behind those zero's there is a "one" (or more)! Such an understanding means accepting the fact that all actions which take place through any body-mind organism are not the acts of any individual entity. Therefore an "insult", for instance, will have no relevance in the absence of a "me."

What is considered "normal" in everyday life is separation. What is not realized is that in such normality exists conflict and unhappiness. So the sage says that unless this separation of "me and mine" from the "not-me and not-mine" is given up, there can be no happiness. And yet this giving up of separation is considered impractical and abnormal. This is where the misconception lies: the human being wants to retain his separation and yet he demands happiness, which is the essential character of the "whole" Consciousness. Indeed this is the basic problem of the seeker. He intuitively feels the oneness of the universe and is deeply aware of the universal pulse of unity. Yet he wishes to experience the happiness of this universal beingness of Noumenality as the separateness of his individual entity in phenomenality. He does not realize that the impersonal sense of presence—the impersonal universal Consciousness—is the normal state and not, as he mistakenly assumes, an aberration or altered state of Consciousness. It is the separation which is an aberration and therefore causes conflict and unhappiness.

The sage says: "Give up all distinction such as 'I am this' and 'I am not this'." The ordinary word in Sanskrit for "give up" is *tyaja*, but the sage uses the word *santyaja*. There is a great deal of difference between the two, *tyaja* means more in the nature of an order or an instruction, whereas *santyaja* implies a sense of faith and conviction, a sense of totality and permanence. In the other verses in this series, the sage tries to impress upon the disciple the intellectual reasons which could help to bring about the transformation from the intellectual understanding to an intuitive conviction. The distinction between the two words is the kind of distinction between the futile personal efforts of an addict to give up his addiction, and the sudden divine urge which impels the giving up of the addiction. The separation between the "me" and the "not-me" is a sort of aberration (an addiction), which needs "outside" help, and the *guru* is the means through which such outside help becomes available at the appropriate time.

There is another more subtle aspect of this matter of "giving-up" (or "letting-go"). There is one kind of giving-up which has, as its basis, the giving up of one thing in order to get something later. But there is a more genuine giving-up where something is given up as being harmful or useless, by itself, not necessarily in exchange for something more acceptable. It is a question of giving up a concept or an illusion out of a conviction about its illusoriness, without any other motive. What the sage is saying is not that giving up the separation between "me" and the "other" will bring about happiness, but simply that when this illusory separation is lost what remains is happiness. In other words, the original state of oneness is happiness, and that separation is a sort of eclipse on that state. With the end of separation, the original state of happiness prevails in its pristine state. It is not a question of giving up a smaller house in order to buy a bigger house!

The sage then proceeds to explain that it is through ignorance that the universe appears to exist, and that other than Consciousness nothing exists. Ignorance means separation. Separation means considering oneself as an independent entity, separate from the rest of the world. The obvious question at this stage would be: how did this basic separation arise? The answer is simple—the first split *arose* because of the split between the observer and the observed, the subject and the object. This split is actually the mechanism necessary for the subjective function of observing or perceiving. This is a simple fact. If this is truly understood in its full intensity, the only possible reaction would be for the eyes to close and the mind to become "vacant"—at least for a few moments, until the observer, (the "me", the mind), arises again as the observer separated from that which is observed. When the time and the place are appropriate, this understanding becomes so deeply ingrained that the individual suddenly disappears as a separate observer, and everything is not observed but *witnessed*. Observing by an individual observer inevitably involves the reaction of comparing and judging what is observed. Impersonal witnessing means Noumenal observing of the phenomenal functioning without any comparing and judging. No distinction is made between the acceptable and the unacceptable, and between the consequential host of other opposites which are really interconnected but are not understood by the concerned individual as such.

Such witnessing is possible only when there is a disidentification from the functioning of phenomenality. Then the significance of the phenomenal manifestation and its functioning as being merely a kind of dream-play, an illusory appearance on the screen of Consciousness, is truly understood. And such understanding is not comprehension by an individual comprehender, but apperception, a dimension totally unrelated to individual comprehension.

This is what the sage means when he tells the disciple:

"O, pure Consciousness that you are! Do not concern yourself with affirmations and negations. Abide in the silence of the eternal bliss that you are, and live happily. Give up conceptualizing altogether. Have no beliefs or concepts of any kind. You are the ever free Consciousness. How can thinking help you in any way?"

Consciousness is all that exists, not aware of itself in this primal state of subjectivity, but aware of itself with the movement "I Am." Along with this awareness in movement arises the totality of manifestation as an appearance within the awareness. The functioning of this manifestation means perceiving the manifestation. Indeed, the very existence of the manifestation depends on its being perceived, and for this reason the basic separation arises, of the perceiver object and the perceived object. But both are objects, and the perceiver does not exist as a subject of the perceived objects. Efforts have been made by both science and organized religion to explain the cause of the arising of the manifestation, but the fact of the matter is that space-time (which is the necessary mechanism for the manifestation to appear and function) simply does not exist. Space-time is a concept, and therefore the manifestation therein must also necessarily be a concept, an illusion, an appearance in Consciousness. The nearest science has come, and can come to the Truth is to say that the manifestation is a self-generated process. Only, this self-generated process happens all the time, here and now whenever there is the sense of presence. When this sense of presence, (being conscious) is not there (as in deep sleep or under sedation), there is no manifestation.

In other words, the only truth is beingness, *here and now*. Any thinking means creating images in mind; it means conceptualizing. Therefore, the sage says, what need can there be for the creation of concepts and images for you who are the very Consciousness in which the manifestation appears. Such understanding is itself peace and happiness. No effort can bring about peace and happiness, because effort can only be made by an individual entity (the "me"), and peace and happiness means the absence of the thinking "me."

Ashtavakra continues with this theme further. He repeatedly points out that the nature of the mind-intellect is to project itself out towards the manifestation and its functioning, towards what is illusory and unreal. So the individual considers himself as a separate entity and constantly engages himself in trying to acquire knowledge about this illusory appearance. He does not realize that his pursuit of knowledge merely means prolonging the ignorance through the continuation of his identification with an illusory entity. Ashtavakra makes it clear that unless this process is reversed and the enquiry has turned inward, the process of dis-identification cannot even begin.

Ashtavakra says:

"You may listen to diverse scriptures, or even give learned discourses on them, but abidance in the Self can riot happen unless all that is forgotten." (146)

"You may keep yourself occupied in work, or enjoy the pleasures of the world, or indulge in meditation, and yet you will find that there is an inner urge towards that primal state which is prior to all phenomenality, in which all desire for phenomenal objects is extinguished." (147)

"All keep exerting themselves, and yet find themselves unhappy. They do not realize that it is this very volitional effort that brings about unhappiness. It is only through this understanding that the blessed one reaches awakening." (148)

"Happiness belongs to none but that master-idler to whom even the natural act of opening and closing of the eyes seems an affliction." (149)

"When the mind is free from pairs of opposites like 'this is done but that is not yet done', it acquires an indifference alike to righteousness, wealth, desire for sensual pleasure, as well as liberation." (150)

"One who has an aversion for sense objects is considered a renunciate, and one who covets them is considered sensual. But one who neither rejects nor covets is unconcerned with them." (151)

This set of verses will shock the traditional seeker who has been conditioned to believe that nothing can be acquired without hard word and personal effort, and this is indeed so in everyday life. Here he is told that he must forget whatever he has learnt, that there is no qualitative difference between work, pleasure and meditation. True happiness (real quietude) consists not in volitional effort to achieve happiness but only in understanding what Self-abidance is, and Self-abidance is not something to be acquired but something which arises spontaneously when the mind is free of the concepts of right and wrong, the acceptable and the unacceptable, and all such pairs of opposites. The sage tells us that enlightenment or Self-abidance is our natural state. It does not need to be acquired. Any personal, volitional effort means only strengthening the ego, the "me", which is itself the obstruction which covers and hides our original state. What is more, the sage assures us that the true understanding of this very fact is all that is necessary for the seeker! When the understanding is true and deep, the question "I have understood what you are saying, but having understood your theory, what do I actually do in everyday life" does not arise. It cannot arise. If it does arise, the understanding has not been either true or deep enough.

Specifically, what is the true understanding? What does it precisely mean? It would be difficult to give a more succinct answer than the statement of the Chinese sage Shen Hui, "Only by avoiding intentions will the mind be rid of objects." In other words, true understanding would be that there is no separate individual entity who can have intentions and therefore there is nobody who can have the choice of decision and action. The true understanding is that the apparent individual entity does not live but is being lived as an instrument through which Consciousness functions. Such an understanding—that the individual entity cannot be the subject of any objects—must necessarily mean that no individual can be the comprehender of any knowledge. When no individual exists, what remains is apperception, enlightenment, understanding.

True understanding comports the realization that it is only the "me" notion, the ego, that can have any intention or volition or will. Indeed, they are all synonyms. There is a misconception that the absence of intention or will or motivation implies phenomenal inaction. All it means is that, in the absence of intention, action cannot stop, action must and will happen, but it will not be volitional action but spontaneous, Noumenal action.

True understanding will also comport the realization that in the absence of any individual comprehender, the true understanding cannot possibly be the result or consequence of effort by a non-existent doer. It can only be a spontaneous arising, a result of the natural tendency of the identified Consciousness, that inner inherent urge towards *dis-identification*.

It is from this viewpoint of the futility of volitional action that the sage makes the stunning statement: Happiness belongs to none but that master-idler to who even the natural action of opening and closing the eyes seems an affliction. What he means to imply is that the continuous action of blinking, if regarded as a volitional act, would have been a real affliction. The process of blinking, the respiratory process, the digestive process and the working of the incredibly complex nervous system are all involuntary functions in the human body-mind organism. They do not need any volitional action by the "me"-notion. To the "master-idler" all actions which take place through his body-mind organism are as involuntary as these processes. He does not consider himself as the individual doer of any actions that take place through his body-mind organism. He is therefore referred to as the "master-idler" by the sage. Such a master-idler merely witnesses (without comparing or judging) everything that happens. All actions that take place through the many body-mind organisms, including his own, are seen as being part of the functioning of Totality

Ramana Maharshi, the great master-idler, was once asked by a visitor why he, the Maharshi, did not do some social service or at least go out and preach his own teaching, instead of merely laying about on his couch. The Maharshi calmly asked him, "How do you know that all that is necessary is not already happening just through my being here?"

You become a master-idler when all sense of personal doership is totally lost. Give up action, give up doing, and you become an idler. Give up the sense of personal doership and let action happen, and you become the master-idler.

The sage begins this series of verses by warning the seeker that the more he learns and talks, the more he adds to his memory, which is the storehouse from which more and more concepts arise. These concepts add to the conditioning which covers the original state of Selfabidance. Self-abidance means the absence of thinking and conceptualizing. In those rare moments when the body is relaxed and the mind is quiescent, there exists a state in which the ego is unaware. Unawareness of the ego is the awareness of the Self. When the "me" is absent, it is the "I"—the universal impersonal "I"—which is present. In everyday living, the human being mistakenly believes that he has the choice of decision and action between alternatives. He spends all his energy worrying about results. It is for this reason that the sage says that the wise man is free from pairs of opposites like "this is done but that remains to be done." It is important to note that his does not mean that the wise man is totally unaware of what is done and what remains to be done. If that were so, he would not be a wise man; he would be a simpleton, a stupid man. The point is that true awareness of what remains to be done leads spontaneously to the necessary action without the intervention of the mind worrying about it. The wise man is also aware that all actions that take place through his body-mind organism are part of the functioning of Totality. They are subject to the limitations of the natural characteristics—physical, mental, temperamental—with which the body-mind was endowed at the moment of conception. The wise man makes efforts without worrying about results because he is aware that he has no choice regarding either.

It is necessary to understand the concept of opposites clearly. Everything in life comes in opposites, and everything one values and chooses is one of a pair of opposites. All dimensions are opposites: inside and outside, up and down, high and low, left and right. Our social and aesthetic values are also in terms of opposites: strong and weak, success and failure, beautiful and ugly. Our sciences and philosophies are also in terms of opposites: ontology is concerned with being and non-being, logic with true and false, and existomology with reality and appearance. Life and living seems to consist of nothing but opposites.

It is only human beings who are concerned with *opposites as a problem*. There are certainly opposites in Nature, but the fact of the matter is that it is human beings who create the separation between big fish and small fish, ripe fruit and unripe fruit, clever animals and dumb animals, loyal animals and undependable animals. Pain and pleasure too exist for animals, but it is not a problem for them: When a dog is in pain, it yelps; when a deer is in danger, it is certainly afraid. But the animal does not regret past pain nor does it fear future danger. The human being is quick to point out that there indeed lies the difference between a dumb animal and an intelligent human being. In this attitude, man forgets that he is not separate from nature, that the endowment of intellect in human beings is itself a gift from Nature. It so happens though that this gift is a dubious one with a double-edged sharpness. It is intellect (conceptualizing) which is the root cause of man's unhappiness. Intellect is responsible for the creation of separation between opposites which are in fact inseparable, in the sense that one cannot exist by itself without the other.

It is the human mind-intellect which refuses to accept the natural interconnectedness of opposites as a fact of life. Life and death become life versus death. Good and evil become good versus evil. Then living becomes one continuous process of choice, and the pursuit of that choice. Intellect does not realize that the separation of opposites is unnatural and means conflict and unhappiness. In not accepting the interrelationship between opposites, it has torn them apart, and human misery is based on this very separation. Intellect does not appreciate the fact that the more one values something, the more obsessed one becomes with the possibility of its loss. The fact of the matter is that the human being is trained and conditioned from its very infancy to choose one against the other, and this cannot be done for the simple reason that it is unnatural. Evil cannot be exterminated, nor can disease be eradicated altogether. When one disease is eradicated, another always takes its place.

The fact of the matter is that in this life, which is based on constant change, it is futile to seek what is considered acceptable to the total exclusion of what is considered unacceptable. Indeed the "acceptable" and the "unacceptable" keep on changing all the time depending on circumstances: Happiness consists in accepting the principle of polarity, accepting that the interrelated opposites are the very basis of both the universe and the movements therein. Life then becomes an art, holding the interrelated opposites in balance. As Lao Tzu puts it, "Knowing the male and keeping the female, one becomes a universal stream; becoming a universal stream, one is not separated from eternal virtue." "Male and female", of course, refers not so much to sex as to the dominant characteristics of the masculine and the feminine. The interrelated opposites, in other words, are like the opposite but inseparable sides of a coin, the poles of a magnet, or the pulse and interval in any vibration.

Until comparatively recently, that is to say, until Newtonian physics (which prevailed for several centuries) was overthrown by modern physics, the idea of the inner unity of opposites was confined only to mystics, mostly Eastern. But now even science has accepted reality as a union of opposites. Thus, for instance, rest and motion are no longer opposites. According to the relativity theory, "each is both." An object for one observer may be at rest whilst for another observer, at the same time, it may be in motion. Similarly, the separation between wave and particle has had to disappear when it was found that in certain circumstance a wave would behave like a particle, and vice versa—so now we have "wavicles." There is now no separation of mass from energy, and the old "opposites" are now seen as two aspects of one reality. This discovery was experienced horrendously by the people of Hiroshima and Nagasaki.

Eastern mystics have long held that a sudden, spontaneous movement (I Am) in Consciousness-at-rest (not aware of itself) gave rise to the entire manifestation. Concurrent with that movement of awareness, the potential energy activated itself, and since then nothing in the universe has been static. Things and events which appear to be separate and irreconcilable such as subject and object, past and future, cause and effect etc. are actually a single vibration. A wave cannot exist except as the unity of crest and trough. As Alfred North Whitehead has comparatively recently put it, "All elements in the universe exist as a vibratory ebb and flow of an underlying energy or activity."

Having said all this about the interrelationship of opposites, the real point will be missed altogether if it is not realized that opposites do not really exist except as a concept. And this is what the sage wants to convey to the disciple. Man's unhappiness rests on the fact that he tries to eradicate one of the opposites—the ugliness, the evil, the weakness, the stupidity. In such attempts, the fact that opposites do not exist at all, other than as a concept, is forgotten. The opposites are an illusion created by the mind-intellect through conceptual separation. As Lao Tzu has said, when you think of beauty as beauty, the ugliness is already there; indeed, what is considered beautiful in one place is considered ugly in another.

As Omar Khayyam has put it:

> *After a momentary silence spake*
> *Some vessel of a more ungainly make;*
> *"They sneer at me for leaning all awry:*
> *What! did the hand then of the Potter shake?"*

Ashtavakra says, "When the mind is free from pairs of opposites like 'this is done and that is not done', it acquires an indifference alike to righteousness, wealth, desire for sensual pleasure, *as well as liberation.*" The sage brings out the important fact that once the separation is seen as a mere concept, all conceptually separated opposites lose their validity. All that now remains is the *impersonal* sense of presence, without any *nama-rupa*, individual name and form—the "I Am."

To quote Omar Khayyam again:

> *"There was the Door to which I found no Key;*
> *Thee was the Veil through which I might not see;*
> *Some little talk awhile of Me and Thee*
> *There was—and then no more of Thee and Me."*

In the absence of thee and me, in the absence of separation, lies true happiness. There is no subject seeking any object, even something called "liberation." The sage clearly tells us that happiness is not some *thing* which an individual can chase and acquire. True happiness exists only when there is no conceptualization.

Ashtavakra proceeds further on the theme of the futility of creating separation between the acceptable and the unacceptable, as opposites:

"Desire is at the root of ignorance, and so long as desire persists, the sense of the acceptable and the unacceptable, which is the branch and sprout of the tree of samsara, *must necessarily continue." (152)*

"Activity begets attachment, abstention from activity generates aversion. Rid of the bondage of opposites, the wise man established in the Self, lives like a child." (153)

"One who is attached to samsara *wants to renounce it in order to free himself from misery. But one who is not attached continues to remain in* samsara *and yet live happily." (154)*

"He who seeks enlightenment as an individual seeker, anti still is identified with the body, is neither a jnani nor a yogi, and suffers misery." (155)

"Unless everything is totally forgotten, you cannot be established in the Self, even if Shiva, Vishnu or Brahma be your preceptor." (156)

The sage begins this series of verses by averring that

desire is at the root of ignorance (and unhappiness). Desire creates opposites of acceptable and unacceptable. The acquiring of what seems acceptable has within itself the seed of the unacceptable because of the fear of losing what has been acquired.

Even in the case of physical illness, knowing the cause of the illness is half the solution. In the case of psychological illness—unhappiness—knowing the cause really needs no other positive action, because psychological illness has no concrete basis. It is a curious fact that a human being goes to a *guru* and seeks some positive solution, like a meditation of some kind, to get rid of the psychological illness of unhappiness. The joke is that the psychological illness is the result of seeking something acceptable and now there is a further seeking being done to remove the result of the first seeking! Along with the seeking for happiness comes the further seeking for a spiritual goal called enlightenment. The seeking continues endlessly until frustration results. It is for this reason that the sage comes out with the straightforward statement that the root cause of the misery in *samsara* (life and living in the world) is "desire" and desire leads to seeking what is at the moment considered acceptable. In other words, the sage says, "Give up wanting what is considered acceptable. Be satisfied with What-Is, without wanting to change it into something better. The better will never end, and the seeking—and the frustration—will never cease.

Desire means discontentment, not being satisfied with What-Is. The basis of desire is time and duration. Psychological pain simply means wanting something that is not there in the present moment or rejecting something that exists in the present moment. What the sage says is simple enough. He says the past is dead and the future is non-existent. What is present is the present moment, the eternal present moment from *which can be* witnessed the illusory movement of the future into the past. The present moment is not between the future and the past, but the constant timeless dimension, outside duration. This has to be so because the flow of time cannot be witnessed except from a position outside of duration. Do not live in the frustrations or successes of the past. Do not live in the projections of fears and hopes of the future. Remain in the present moment and you will not be concerned with either happiness or unhappiness. The "within" is the Kingdom of God, the Kingdom of Heaven. It does not need to be "sought" as an object, by any human object.

Finally, Ashtavakra frees the disciple from the ultimate bondage of the *guru* himself. He declares that everything that is gathered intellectually must drop because, other than the impersonal sense of presence (I Am) everything is conceptual. Says the sage, "unless everything (acquired phenomenally) is totally forgotten, you cannot be established in the Self, even if *Shiva* or *Vishnu* or *Brahma* were to be your preceptor."

In *Thus Spake Zarathushtra*, by Frederick Nietzsche, Zarathushtra gives his disciples the ultimate message: Whatever had to be said has been said; whatever had to be understood has been understood. Now forget whatever has been said. Forget everything I have said except this last message. Beware of Zarathushtra!

Unless the individuality is totally lost, how can there be enlightenment? Enlightenment means the annihilation of individuality. Seeking begins with the individual but ends with the annihilation of the individual. Enlightenment can never be a personal achievement. Enlightenment is an impersonal event in phenomenality.

Literature over the last several centuries has as one of its main themes, the cause of unhappiness. Unhappiness has been traced to an astonishing variety of sources from heredity to upbringing to Satan. But it really needs only a little quiet thinking—and this is what the sage points to—to make it clear that there is indeed a single cause of human unhappiness. It is the *"me"-concept*, the notion of a separate individual as the subject with the rest of the world as its object. Desire, greed, envy, pride, ambition etc., which are variously described as the causes of man's unhappiness, all take root from this basic misconception of the individual self. Happiness is truly represented only by the universal presence which knows no "me" as an individual, the impersonality of Consciousness which arrives only with the annihilation of the "me" as a separate doer.

The search, the seeking for pure happiness—the spiritual seeking—begins with the individual. First, an outside compelling urge turns the mind inward. Then the process of disidentification begins with the identified individual either going to a *guru*, and/or starting to read up on the subject. With the urge driving the seeker relentlessly, he does an enormous amount of reading and acquires what he considers a great deal of knowledge (and along with it considerable pride as a seeker). What actually has been happening, however, is that during all this time, during all this reading, only those statements of "truth" are accepted which fit in with the seeker's conditioned notions. He has conveniently rejected (consciously or unconsciously) all those which he did not like or understand. The result is a patchwork of personal philosophy, armed with which, the seeker gets more and more anxious to reform the world. It is this "knowledge" which the sage says must be "forgotten", which must drop off before anything worthwhile can happen. Unless this ignorance in the garb of knowledge gets thrown out, says the sage, you cannot be established in the Self, "even if Shiva, Vishnu or Brahma be your preceptor."

In the course of spiritual evolution, the seeker, at the appropriate time, realizes that that which he had been regarding as knowledge is really nothing but ignorance. He then strips off these clothes of conceptual knowledge, goes naked to a Self-realized *guru* (more accurately, happens to be led by circumstances to the appropriate *guru*) who clothes him in garments of true understanding. It is only then that the urge fulfills itself and the process—the impersonal process—of the disidentification of the identified Consciousness is completed.

CHAPTER EIGHT

✤

Having explained how true understanding comes about only after ignorance in the form of conceptual knowledge is given up, Ashtavakra now proceeds to describe the state of the true knower of Truth:

"It is only he who is contented, with his senses not attached to their objects and who revels in his oneness with the universe, who can be considered as having become a jnani and a yogi." (157)

"0, the Knower of Truth never experiences misery in this world, for the whole universe is filled by himself." (158)

"The sense-objects no longer have any attraction for the one who abides in the Self, just as the bitter leaves of the neem tree cannot please an elephant who can enjoy the sallaki leaves." (159)

"Rare in the world is the one on whom experiences do not leave any impressions, and who does not hanker after any experiences still to be enjoyed." (160)

"It is possible to find in this world those who crave sensual gratification and also those who hanker after enlightenment. But rare indeed is the great soul who cares neither for material enjoyment nor spiritual enlightenment." (161)

"The man of wisdom does not wish for the dissolution of the universe, nor is he interested in its continuance. The blessed one lives perfectly contented with whatever turns up in life." (163)

What Ashtavakra says seems simple enough, and it has a much deeper significance which is likely to escape a mere cursory, superficial hearing. The sage says, "It is only he who is contented, with his senses not attached to their objects, and who revels in his oneness with the universe, who can be considered as having become a *jnani* and a *yogi*." There is a distinct possibility of the cause and effect being misunderstood unless the verse is given careful thought. The general impression—and the general teaching—is that in order to "achieve" enlightenment, "one" must be contented, possess dispassion and enjoy being alone. What the sage is saying is that contentment, dispassion and self-abidance are the result or consequences of the happening of enlightenment. Being alone does not bring about enlightenment. When enlightenment happens, meditation happens in which there is no individual meditator. Self-abidance happens too, in the sense that no need is felt of any companionship. It must be understood that such selfabidance does not mean that companionship becomes unacceptable. What it means is that if the *jnani* has company, he participates in whatever happens without any involvement, merely witnessing whatever happens. When there is nothing to witness, the senses do not run out to their objects. The mind turns inward and meditation happens. This is the state which Ramana Maharshi calls the natural state (*sahaja sthiti*). Consciousness prevails but the response of the senses to sound, smell etc. is extremely passive. This non-witnessing state (when there is nothing to witness) and the witnessing state (when something is happening) alternate very smoothly in the case of the *jnani* according to the need of the moment. It is like unconsciously shifting gears in an automobile according to the needs of the traffic.

What this means really is that it is not necessary to go to a forest in order to get enlightenment. You can be in your normal circumstances and go about your normal life and still get enlightened if there is true understanding. The understanding is that every individual human being, as part of the totality of manifestation, is merely the objective expression of the unmanifest subject. As such, he can never possibly have any individual volition to decide and act as a separate doer. Enlightenment does not come about *because* you have given up your wife and family and wealth. What does happen is that when through a true understanding enlightenment does occur, attachment to these objects will disappear. Objects are not an obstruction, only attachment to the objects is an obstruction. Attachment to the sense objects drops off only when there is a conviction that the entire manifestation and its functioning is a dream-play. Until there is such conviction it is futile to try to give up anything. When will such conviction arise? Only when sense objects have been completely enjoyed and the hollowness of such enjoyment has been realized. Deliberate suppression of desires is futile because it is necessarily the "me" who "decides" to give them up. When the illusoriness of the "me" itself is realized, the whole perspective and the entire attitude gets changed.

What the *jnani* revels in is not one's aloneness but the oneness of the universe. Aloneness means loneliness. Oneness is felt even in a crowd when the separation of "me" and the "other" is not there. In fact, there is no question really of loneliness or aloneness because there is truly no "one" to feel lonely or alone. The "me" and along with it the "other" is just a concept. No one sees or hears. There is only seeing and hearing. The seeing and the seen, the hearing and the heard have nothing personal about them. Both are impersonal Consciousness. The understanding of this one fact brings about the understanding of the oneness of the universe, which is impersonality. Enlightenment means the recession of the illusory person into impersonality.

What the sage is saying in these verses is that what characterizes the "wise man", the "rare one", the "great soul" is the fact that he lives in this world as if he is not in it. In other words, he lives in this world as if he is acting a role in a dream-play. The sense objects no longer attract him. Experiences do not leave any impression on him. He neither craves for sensual gratification nor hankers after spiritual awakening. He is indifferent to the various motivations in life—*dharma, artha, kama, moksha.* He is in fact not even concerned whether he lives or dies.

What does all this mean? It means simply that there is no individual "me" at all. Hence the words "Selfabidance" and "oneness of the universe." It means that the awakened sage thinks and lives vertically in a world of *karma* that moves horizontally. Horizontal movement is the stream of time, in which every action becomes a cause to be followed by a reaction or effect. For the sage, the split-mind of the individual person has been healed into the wholeness of impersonality. No experience, no event gets recorded into any particular individual reaction, and this kind of inaction of the sage is obviously not intelligible to the average person. The average person is bound by *karma*—action/reaction, cause/effect—whereas the awakened sage is free from a particular reaction. Indeed, it is the vertical vision (the impersonal witnessing of all events) of the sage which is the *consequence of the true understanding*, the liberation from the bondage of *karma.* Such vertical seeing and living cannot be practiced as a method. It is only identified individuals who are interested in a practicable method to achieve some object. All that is needed is an *understanding as such*, without the presence of an individual comprehender.

When the understanding is clear that all there is, is Consciousness, the universe and every thing in it, including human beings, cease to have any significance. It is in relevance to this fact that the sage says that "the man of wisdom does not wish for the dissolution, nor is he interested in its continuance." Life and death to him are meaningless terms. So long as life continues, and the body-mind organism is functioning, he lives perfectly contented from day to day with whatever turns up at the moment.

Ashtavakra continues:

"In consequence of this supreme understanding, with the split-mind healed into its wholeness, the wise one lives happily in contentment, seeing, hearing, touching, smelling and tasting." (164)

"He has neither attachment nor aversion for objects in this world, and so, is not buffeted about in the sea of samsara. His mind is vacant, his actions are without personal motivation, and his senses are not attracted to their objects. (165)

"The wise one neither keeps awake nor does he sleep, and his eyes are neither open nor closed. The liberated soul enjoys the state in any circumstances." (166)

"The liberated one is found to be always abiding in the Self. Pure in heart, he lives free of all conditioning in any circumstances." (167)

"Seeing, hearing, touching, smelling, tasting, accepting, speaking, walking, the great-souled one, free from all effort and non-effort, is indeed emancipated." (168)

"The liberated one neither abuses nor praises. He neither rejoices, nor is he angry. He neither gives nor receives. He is free from attachment to any object." (169)

"The sight of a voluptuous woman or that of approaching death leaves the great-souled one, established in the Self, equally unperturbed. He is indeed liberated." (170)

"The steady one who sees the same everywhere, does not differentiate between happiness and misery, man and woman, prosperity and adversity." (171)

"In the wise one whose attachment to worldly life has been exhausted, you will find neither compassion, nor violence, neither humility nor insolence, neither wonder nor excitement." (172)

"The liberated one neither abhors objects of the senses, nor does he covet them. He enjoys whatever comes along, with a perfectly detached mind." (173)

"Always abiding in the Self, the wise one of vacant mind does not conceptualize on the opposites like right and wrong, good and evil." (174)

"Devoid altogether o f the feeling of "me" and "mine", knowing with firm conviction that no thing exists in reality, and with all his inner desires set at rest, the man of understanding does not act, though it may appear that he is acting." (175)

"It is an indescribable state that comes to the man of understanding, whose mind has melted away and conceptualizing has ceased, and who is totally free from delusion, dreaming and dullness." (176)

The sage conveys beautifully the transformation that has taken place. As Jnaneshwar put it two thousand years later, the split-mind has healed into its wholeness when you are able to see your face without the aid of the mirror. As a Chinese sage, the Sixth Patriarch Hui Neng revealed the Truth to his persecutor, "When you do not think good and when you do not think not-good, what is your true Self (original face)?" Anything that was seen as acceptable or unacceptable, pleasant or unpleasant, better or worse, was a judgement dictated by the splitmind of the me-concept. Whenever such judging was eliminated, the me-concept was absent, and what remained would be the whole-mind, the original face.

The supreme understanding happens with the realization that there is nothing to look for. Indeed when you look for It, It disappears, and when you cease to look for It, you cannot escape It. The wise one lives happily in contentment, seeing, hearing, touching, smelling and tasting, with the full realization that it is the Unmanifest in that which he sees, hears, touches, smells and tastes. Every sensory and conceptual experience is an illusion. "It" is the within of the without with which we are surrounded on all sides, the within which is the Kingdom of God, the pure Consciousness, the Unmanifest from which everything manifests but not as separate things.

The wise man is fully aware of the identity between *samsara* and *nirvana*. In the whole-mind of the wise man *samsara* is seen as *nirvana* in objective expression, while at the same time he knows that both are concepts and, as such, neither exists. What the ordinary person does is to separate the two and then to attempt to see *nirvana* through the split-mind of *samsara* and hence gets "buffeted about in the sea of *samsara*." The wise man is aware that he is no longer an object misbelieving itself to be the subject of other objects because he has disidentified himself (more accurately, disidentification has taken place) from the role of separated subject. In such disidentifcation the wise man merely witnesses all that happens without any personal involvement. And when there is nothing to witness, there is the state of non-witnessing.

The way of life for the awakened or the wise man, that the sage has described, may be said to be free living or happy living or Noumenal living. Its basis is the clear realization that a so-called individual, as a mere instrument, cannot possibly live according to his own sweet will and pleasure. He is being lived as a dreamed character in this living dream. Neither the character in a personal dream nor a character in this living world can live as a separate personal entity. Both are puppets merely responding to outside impulses, events over which they have no control. An unconditional acceptance of this fact means living in freedom. Then there are no restrictions by way of volition and the exercise of it (making choices). In such living there is neither past nor future, neither attraction nor rejection, neither sleep nor waking, because all these are conceptual conditions based on time whereas the awakened being always lives in the present moment.

In this free living (Noumenal living) there does not arise any question of grasping anything. Whatever comes along is accepted unconditionally (all reactions being completely spontaneous, without any personal involvement). What does not come along is not missed or hankered after. Whatever happens is merely witnessed. Is this not true freedom, freedom from the bondage of volition? The bondage of volition is felt every time there is the feeling of not wanting to make a choice; wishing one did not have to make a decision. Freedom is the relief from the worry over consequences of choices and decisions. Such total freedom is the result of unequivocally accepting "Not my will but Thine, 0 Lord", the basis of all the teachings of all the Masters of all the schools of liberation. Acceptance is not total if the "me" continues to make deliberate, personal efforts to "achieve" anything, including enlightenment. Acceptance is indeed total when all actions that take place through all body-mind organisms (including one's own) are accepted as the functioning of Totality, the expression of "Thy will."

The actual living of a sage, because of its very naturalness, its apparent ordinariness, often goes unnoticed inspite of the fact that he usually deals with social and practical matters with extraordinary smoothness. His is a kind unselfconscious elegance, an uncontrived skill.

The sage says that the mind, the attitude (the gaze), of the wise man of understanding is "vacant." What the sage means is that it appears to the ordinary person as vacant because his own gaze (attitude) is always colored by a judging of whatever he perceives as being beautiful or ugly, good or evil etc. The man of understanding however, perceives everything as his own reflection, as the objective expression of the subjective Noumenon.

❧

CHAPTER NINE

☙

In the next one hundred verses, Ashtavakra gives a summary and rounds off the teaching. Ashtavakra continues:

"Salutations to that which is the embodiment Of Bliss, Serenity, Effulgence, with the dawn of knowledge of which all delusion becomes like a dream." (177)

"One can get a great deal of pleasure through the acquisition of the manifested sense objects. It is, however, only through the renunciation of all, that happiness can arrive." (178)

The poet sage Bhartrihari wrote two books, one called *A Hundred Verses on Enjoyment*, and the other *A Hundred Verses on Renunciation*. In the latter, he says:

"Enjoyment is always accompanied by the fear of misery, social position is always accompanied by the fear of a downfall, wealth by the fear of loss, honor by the fear of humiliation, power by the fear of foes, physical beauty by the fear of old age, scriptural erudition by the fear of fresh opponents, virtue by the fear of seduction, life by the fear of death. All the things of the world pertaining to human beings are attended with fear. Renunciation alone eliminates all fear."

> "How can one, the core of whose very being has been scorched by the heat o f the Sun o f Sorrow arising from a sense of duty, enjoy happiness without the continuous ambrosial showers of desirelessness?" (179)

> "This universe is but a state of Consciousness. In reality it is nothing. The inherent nature of the Existent and the Non-existent is never lost." (180)

> "The Self, the Absolute—effortless, immutable, taintless—is neither far away nor subject to limitation. It is always there, ever present." (181)

> "As soon as illusion ceases, the intervening obstruction of the vision is removed. When the pure understanding shines, the miseries are dispelled." (182)

> "Knowing that everything that appears is a figment of the imagination, and that what is eternal and independent is the subjective Self as Consciousness, is it possible for the enlightened being to act foolishly like a child?" (183)

It is as if Ashtavakra suddenly realized that he was in the previous verses, attempting to show subjectivity from the object's point of view. It is in fact, rather absurd to try to perceive *nirvana* from the angle of *samsara*. To seek anything *non-samsaric* through the *samsaric* split-mind of the individual is futile because from that direction the true nature of *nirvana* can never be *known*, it can only be a concept.

The sage therefore begins the series with offering salutations to That, the knowledge of which causes all delusion to disappear. With that knowledge, the delusion of seeing this living dream as real itself seems like a dream. When the understanding dawns, the immediate reaction is the surprise that there should have been a delusion at all! On awakening, the earlier delusion appears like a dream.

The word used for "salutations" is *"namah"*, the root of which is *namana*, which means bending in obeisance. The significance of this is humility, not as the opposite of pride but as the absence of an entity which can be proud or humble. When the river enters the sea, it offers salutations to the ocean by erasing its own individuality and merging with the ocean. In fact, the extinction of the "me" as an entity is indeed enlightenment since there remains no "one" to even desire enlightenment.

There is truly no mystery about That. The mystery is created by the individual "me" through the totally futile effort to see its own phenomenal absence. That cannot hide anywhere because it is pure presence, here-now, all the time everywhere. That, as Consciousness, is all there is, other than That nothing is. That, as pure subjectivity, is without the slightest trace of objectivity, and it is for this reason that the individual seeker cannot find it. It is That Consciousness which exists as each being, but not as That. When we look for That, we cannot find it because it is That which we are, not this (psychosomatic organism) which we *think* we are. Words cannot make this clear, and it was therefore that one Master instructed a disciple, "Do not let yourself be put out by a *sutra*, put out the *sutra* instead!" Words can only be pointers, but we have perforce to use them until that is unnecessary. Once the sense can be maintained, the words must be abandoned.

That, our real nature, is not something inaccessible, a far-off will-o-the-wisp that we are apt to conceive. In fact it is no thing to be conceived. It is *nothing*. It is the within of the without that we mistakenly believe to be real. It is the unmanifest of that which our senses consider as manifest. It is the reality of every conceptual and sensual experience that is really an illusion. It is the negative of everything we consider as positive. All that is necessary is for us to cease to attempt to become something (perhaps enlightened) or to achieve something (even enlightenment). And then there we are in our true nature, pure Consciousness which is all there is, all there was, and all there ever will be: I Am.

All that is necessary for the awareness of our real nature to happen, is for the cloak of our *persona* (the mask) to drop off. The wanting and the desiring must fall off. And then what remains in that nakedness is the nothingness, the void (or plenum), our transparent real nature of bliss, serenity, effulgence. This is what is envisaged when the sage talks of "renunciation." He does not mean deliberately giving up or suppressing anything. When someone talks of giving up something, apart from the nearly tangible sense of pride in the possession of the necessary strength to give it up, you will invariably notice that there is a motive behind such "sacrifice." One gives up something in order to gain something else. This is not the kind of renunciation the sage is thinking of. Behind every kind of deliberate renunciation, there is motivation, and behind motivation there is inevitably the "me" entity. What is necessary for awakening to take place is the falling off of this very "me" entity. It is only when the true understanding dawns that our true nature has no needs (that needs concern only the body) that true renunciation *happens*.

What is true renunciation? Of all the things that must be given up—acquired knowledge, built-in conditioning, continually increasing demand for more and more of everything etc.—perhaps the most important would be the notion that one lives one's own life. It would be a futile gesture to give up everything else and then persist in believing that it is possible for one to live one's own life. One must go deeply enough into the matter to realize unequivocally that one cannot really live one's life because one is in fact being lived all the time. We have had no choice in being born, and we certainly do not have anything to say about our death, and yet we have the temerity to say that in between these two phenomena of birth and death, during the intermediate period, we have the choice to live as we like, do what we like.

Here is what the Arabian sage Monoimus has to say on the matter:

"Learn whence is sorrow and joy, and love and hate, and waking though one would not, and sleeping though one would not, and falling in love when one would not. And if thou shouldst closely investigate all these things, thou wilt find God in thyself, one and many, just as the atom; thus finding in thyself a way out of thyself."

Once it is seen that volition is in fact illusory, it becomes clear that, in order to see something which is already there, no effort is necessary by way of disciplines, practices or devices such as any repeated affirmations of formulae, or thoughts or words. The Taoist philosophy calls all effort to realize the Tao as "putting legs on a snake" because "everything is Tao."

Ashtavakra carries the question of volition into the realm of duty (and righteousness), and says that the sense of duty (and righteousness) is the very antithesis of happiness. The word used is the sanskrit word "*kartavya*." It means something that should be done (which is, of course, a concept), an aspect of doing other than the triad of the deed, the doing and the doer. To this extent, the word *kartavya* clearly implies a sense of duty or righteousness. That is to say the word implies volition and intention. It is the sense of doership which brings about the pleasure of achievement together with the misery of failure. The sage says the tension is increased with the notion of duty and righteousness. With such continuous tension in life (never really knowing what is right or wrong in the prevailing circumstances), how can there be happiness, the sage asks.

Non-rational creatures, as Aldous Huxley put it, live in the animal eternity of a perpetual present. Instinct is their animal grace and constant inspiration. They are not worried about right and wrong. They are never tempted to live otherwise than in accord with their own animal *dharma*, or immanent law. The human being, on the other hand, relies on personal cleverness (reasoning) rather than on instinct and intuition. And this is what Nature has intended. This "wearisome condition of humanity" is a prerequisite of enlightenment. Cleverness and reason "are not and cannot be a proximate means of union with God." They are, however, necessary to bring about first, the intellectual understanding of our real nature that could lead to a deeper understanding in the heart. And what has been happening is that cleverness and reason has been leading humanity not to spirituality but to technology and "progress." Advises Jalal-uddin Rumi: sell your cleverness and buy bewilderment; cleverness is mere opinion, bewilderment is intuition. The fact of the matter is that such transaction can take place only at the appropriate time, when the realization dawns that the human being does not live, but is being lived.

It must be noted that the word the sage uses is "*kartavya*" (which is the cause of unhappiness), and not *dharma*. "*Dharma*" originally was used in the Indian formulation of the perennial philosophy as the essential nature of any thing, the innate principle of its being. Later on however, *dharma* has acquired the meaning of righteousness and piety, involving an interpretation of what is right and wrong. Ashtavakra says that the misery caused by such interpretation of what should be done and what should not be done can be countered only by desirelessness. What the sage says is that volitional living means misery, non-volitional living means happiness.

What is non-volitional living? Non-volitional living is what happens when the arrogant and silly notion that we live our own lives has fallen off, when thereby all that is to be renounced has fallen off, not one by one, but *en bloc*. Strictly speaking, therefore, there can never be any non-volitional living in the same sense that any deliberate not-doing is also an act of doing. The term is not intended to mean the positive act of living volitionally or non-volitionally but rather accepting that we are being lived as part of the functioning of Totality. Indeed, volition is merely a concept and not an effective operating element at all in phenomenal living. Volition is merely an expression of the me-concept, pretending to interfere in the process of causation, the cause-effect chain. The result is a sense of satisfaction if the effect is acceptable, and of misery if it is unacceptable. Needless to say, the acceptability or otherwise of any event has no real, firm base in itself. It varies from time to time according to circumstances.

Non-volitional living, in other words, means direct living, spontaneous living. It is living without unnecessarily bringing into the cause-effect process a sense of personal will or intention. Such direct, spontaneous living cannot be the result of the personal efforts of any fictitious, illusory "me." It can only be the result of a sudden, deep understanding arising from dis-identification with a spurious entity. It is an effect of in-seeing. Indeed, such spontaneous, direct living is the very expression of the understanding in daily life. It is not, as Alan Watts put it, "virtue in the sense of moral rectitude, with which the enlightened being is quite unconcerned, but becomes essentially the *dharma* of that being, without conscious direction, like the fruition of plants, the formation of eyes and ears, the circulation of blood and the reticulation of nerves, indeed like the growth of the fetus in the womb."

"With the firm conviction that one's real nature is Consciousness, and that existence and non-existence are alike figments of the imagination, can there be anything for the one who is without desires, to think, or to say, or to do?" (184)

"For the yogi who has become silent through the certain knowledge that all there is is Consciousness, all thought such as "I am this" or "I am not that", is extinguished." (185)

"The yogi who is perfect in serenity is concerned neither with distraction nor with concentration, neither with knowledge nor with ignorance, neither with pleasure nor with misery." (186)

"For the yogi whose conditioning has totally dropped off, riches or poverty, gain or loss, being among people or in the solitude of the forest, is a matter of complete indifference." (187)

"For the yogi who has transcended dualities such as "this is completed" and "that is still to be completed", how can there be any question of duty, wealth, sense-enjoyment, or discrimination?" (188)

In these verses, the sage describes the non-volitional, direct, spontaneous living of the enlightened being.

The word *"yogi"* used by the sage in these verses needs some explanation because it is likely to be misinterpreted as someone who has *achieved* Self-realization through yogic practices and disciplines. The sage makes it clear repeatedly that by *yogi* he means the one who has transcended the duality of opposites and who has the knowledge, with total certainty and conviction of the illusoriness of both existence and non-existence. One is reminded of the description of that quantum jump from objectivity to subjectivity, that complete transformation, the *metanoesis*, the *para-vritti*, given by Master Kao Feng: At that moment my doubts were suddenly broken up: I felt as if I had jumped out of a trap. All the puzzling *koans* of the Masters and the Buddhas and all the different issues and events of both present and ancient times became transparently clear to me. Henceforth all things were settled; nothing under the sun remained but peace.

The sage uses the words "understood with certainty" or "understood with great conviction" in order to make it clear that the understanding, if intellectual or conceptual, is not "certain" knowledge. He is confirming the saying, "to acquire understanding at the hands of others is to close the gates of Self-enlightenment." Understanding acquired at the hands of others is necessarily objective understanding. In objective science somebody else's understanding, if correct, would be perfectly valid for you and me, and could be transferred to us. But the understanding that the sage speaks of, cannot be transferred or transmitted. Phenomenal, dualistic pointers from Masters could lead you within "sight" of it, but the actual "seeing" of it must happen to "you" yourself. Strictly speaking, the "sight" and the "seeing" and the "you" are, of course, inaccurate, but the sense should be obvious.

It is for this reason that many seekers, after years of conscientiously doing all the prescribed practices and disciplines, end up in frustration. Behind all practices and disciplines there is the "me"-concept, wanting something. Understanding with conviction, (in-seeing), can happen only in the total absence of the "me." The Master can only lead you to the illusory gate, the gateless gate at the end of the pathless path. It is only in the effortless silence of the phenomenal void (which is the Noumenal plenum) that the leap can take place and the transformation happen.

The point still needs to be cleared up: to whom does this understanding happen? In whom does this conviction take place? The only answer is that so long as this question remains, the true understanding with certainty and conviction will not have taken place. The question remains only for someone who has yet to be blessed with the understanding. The happening of the understanding is coincident with the annihilation of the "me", and so then none remains to ask the question. Such depth of understanding is apperception. It is an understanding and perception that is prior to both knowledge and ignorance. It is beyond the opposites of logic and reason. It is beyond concepts and beliefs. This conviction arises in that silence in which all concepts and beliefs and doubts merge and get annihilated. It is only in that silence that there is relief from the comparison of opposites (known as mentation or thinking) that is the activity of the split-mind of intellect.

The sage expresses in one verse the entire philosophy of non-duality. He says with firm conviction that existence and non-existence are both figments of imagination. What can there be to think, or to say, or to do? Existence and non-existence, appearance and non-appearance, are all figments of imagination. What does this mean? Existence means objective existence and there can be objective existence only because objects are sensorially perceivable by us. Metaphysically, not-existing would be a form of existing, just as not-doing would be a form of doing. In the absence of perceiving there would be no existence. Existence, therefore, depends upon the object being perceived. But the perceptive faculty itself is an objective concept in Consciousness, existing only in the relation that depends upon the existence of the object perceived. The perceiver object and the perceived object being both objects, we could not perceive or conceive anything without something which had the faculty of conceiving, something that transcends both. And this that transcends both existence and non-existence is Consciousness or *Brahman*. And this is what is known or apperceived in a dimension totally different from knowing and not-knowing in phenomenality. To put the whole matter differently, the appearance and the non-appearance are both in consciousness, and therefore, as the sage says, are figments of the imagination. The manifestation does not exist (or not exist) when consciousness is absent as in the case of deep sleep or under sedation. Therefore, when it is clearly seen that the "me"-concept is illusory, and that all there is, is Consciousness, "who" can be there to think anything, or say anything, or do anything?

In the briefest way, what the sage conveys is that what you think you are and what you think you are not are both concepts. It is only when the "me"-concept exists that the concept of *Thee* (as not-me) has relevance. In the silence of the void both concepts disappear.

For one who is without desires, can there by anything to think, or to say, or to do? It is not that there are no thoughts or that nothing is said or that nothing is done. Whatever thoughts take place, whatever gets said and whatever gets done, happens naturally and spontaneously through the body-mind organism as the instrument. There is no separate entity who considers himself as the thinker, as the sayer or the doer. It is in this sense that the Buddha after having walked and talked almost all the time for forty-two years, is said not to have walked a step or uttered a single word. All thoughts, words and deeds happened naturally and spontaneously as part of the functioning of Totality. Once the real nature of the manifest and the unmanifest is realized as the impersonal Consciousness, desires evaporate and there remains no volitional motivation to think or say or do anything other than that which happens spontaneously. These actions—and their consequence, if any, -will be part of the functioning of Totality.

The sages say that the disidentification with any separate entity brings about the conviction that all there is, is Consciousness. With this conviction arises the supreme sense of contentment and peace. All the causes of confusion and discontentment—desire, greed, envy, pride etc.—are not independent phenomena but merely the manifestations of the identified ego. It is important to understand this. It is only because this is not clearly apprehended in its depth—though it might have been superficially comprehended by the mind—that people visit "godmen." They ask those "godmen" to show them the way to get rid of the confusion and conflict in which they find themselves all the time. In a way this is a real joke inasmuch as they want the identified "me" to enjoy something which can come about only when the "me" disappears. It is even more of a joke that such "seekers" go to such great lengths, not only spending a lot of money on religious rituals, but often going in for quite strenuous physical and mental disciplines and practices. In the end all these efforts result in frustration because the very basis of such practices is the "me"-concept *wanting something.*

It is interesting to note that Ashtavakra has clearly stated that deliberate sitting in meditation ultimately cannot bring about an understanding. It may produce temporary benefits but these only induce an indulging in meditation, and the sage warns that such indulging in meditation is an obstruction to the dawning of understanding. It is also interesting to note that St. John of the Cross, an enlightened Christian, defines deliberate meditation as "discursive mental activity by means of images, forms and figures that are produced imaginatively", and considers such meditation as "the first thing to be got rid of."

It is as if the sage is ticking off point after point, one pair of opposites after another, in order to show that having seen the illusoriness of one pair of opposites, all the others become irrelevant. Having understood the illusoriness of the very base of all pairs of opposites, that is the "me" concept as a separate entity, it hardly needs any thought for the illusoriness of the pairs of opposites to be clearly seen. The *yogi* who is in perfect serenity, says the sage, is concerned with neither distraction nor concentration, which along with knowledge and ignorance, pleasure and pain are the conditions of the mind. When the mind says that one knows something or does not know something there is That which knows that one knows or one does not know. There is necessarily That which cognizes that there is distraction or concentration, that there is pleasure or pain. That cognizing element is What-We-Are, not the split-mind of the "me" which interprets the event as acceptable or unacceptable. When such interpretation by the split-mind is not there, as in the case of the sage, one abides in the Self. As the understanding dawns, there are frequent moments of serenity when the interpreting split-mind does not intrude upon the consciousness. When the understanding deepens, such moments become longer and more frequent, until finally enlightenment happens and the sage gets born.

When you deliberately sit for *dhyana*, you will find yourself being disturbed and thereby getting upset by every little thing like the ringing of the telephone or the barking of the dogs, and you will start grumbling and thinking of ways and means to get rid of the nuisance. When, however, the understanding suddenly and spontaneously peeps through into consciousness, and the eyes close by themselves and a sense of peace descends into spontaneous meditation, the situation is a different dimension altogether. The distraction does not matter; neither does concentration because the "one" who creates the difference is absent. For such a yogi for whom seeking has ceased altogether, who accepts life as it comes along, neither hankering after anything nor shirking anything, it matters little whether he is amidst prosperity or amidst poverty, whether he is in the company of people or in the solitude of a forest, whether some event brings gain or loss. He lives in the present eternal moment and witnesses everything as a passing show. Witnessing of everything that gets done simply happens, since there is no involvement with what is done as something done by himself, there is no involvement with what remains to be done. And without any worry on this score, possibly much more gets done than would otherwise have been the case. In a way this has a similarity to what Lao Tzu means when he says, "Superior virtue uses no force, but nothing is left undone. Inferior virtue uses force, but achieves nothing."

For the sage, says Ashtavakra, where is the question of righteousness or duty, or worldly possessions or sensual enjoyment or discrimination? All these terms are merely labels for concepts and have no relevance in his natural way of life. To quote Lao Tzu once again, "superior virtue is not intentionally virtuous and thus is virtue; inferior virtue does not let go of being virtuous, and thus is not virtue." The sage's grace in living comes naturally through his intuitive realization of oneness of the objective manifestation and the subjective unmanifest.

Ashtavakra continues in the same strain:

"For the liberated sage there is neither duty nor attachment. All his actions form part of his non-volitional way of living." (189)

"For the sage who is beyond all conceptualization, where is the question of delusion or the universe and its renunciation, or the matter of liberation itself?" (190)

"He who perceives the universe as universe may have to deny its existence. But he who is without concepts is not concerned with it. He perceives it, and yet does not see it." (191)

"He who perceives the Brahman as something separate from himself may have to meditate on the principle "I am Brahman." But he who has transcended all conceptualization and thus sees nothing as other than himself, has nothing to meditate upon." (192)

"He who experiences distraction in himself finds it necessary to control such distractions, but what is therefor the noble-minded man to do, who has not identified himself with any distractions?" (193)

"The sage appears to live like any ordinary person, but there is a fundamental difference in their outlooks. The sage knows that all there is, is Consciousness, and therefore does not concern himself with either concentration or distraction." (194)

"Having transcended the relative concept of existence and non-existence, the man of understanding, contented and free from desire, does absolutely nothing even though in the eyes of the world he goes about his business." (195)

"The sage is content to do whatever he is expected to be doing in his particular circumstance, but is not really involved either in the doing or the non-doing of it." (196)

All these verses bring out one basic fact: the sage has realized that there is a body but it is not his body, nor is he the body; there are thoughts, but they are not his thoughts, nor is he the thoughts; there are desires, but they are not his desires, nor is he the desires; there are emotions, but they are not his emotions, nor is he the emotions. The sage has apperceived beyond the shadow of a doubt that what there is, after all thoughts, desires, feelings and emotions have been merely witnessed, is a pure center of awareness which has no taint of personality. In fact the fundamental realization is that there is no thing other than Consciousness, and therefore there is no question of any one (or any thing) identifying himself with anything or dis-identifying himself from something else. As Ashtavakra says, he who perceives the *Brahman* as something separate from himself may have to meditate on the principle "I am *Brahman*", but he who has transcended all conceptualization and thus sees nothing as other then himself, has nothing to meditate upon.

What does all this ultimately mean? Through all these verses, the sage is hammering only one point: The perceiver cannot be the perceived; what is perceived cannot be the perceiver. Phenomenally, the perceived and the perceiver are both objects, therefore, the perceiving element, the subjective element, must necessarily be That which is not objective, something different from the perceiving mechanism. It must be that same element which does the perceiving through the billions of body-mind organisms. That subjective perceiving element, Consciousness, being all there is, where is the question of identification or dis-identification, except, of course, notionally. The danger in trying to understand anything notionally is that the notion is likely to be understood as reality. Nonetheless, intellectual understanding may begin with the notion that ignorance is the identification of the Perceiver with the mechanism of perceiving, that bondage is the mis-identification of the perceiving element (the real "perceiver") with all that can be perceived, and that therefore, liberation means dis-identification from the perceiving mechanisms and all that can be perceived.

When the universe has been apperceived as an illusion,

the perceiver has already become part of the illusion and so there remains no "one" to conceptualize, no one to meditate on any delusion or bondage or liberation. There remains no one to deny the existence or non-existence of the universe. There remains no one to meditate on his real nature. There remains no one to feel any distractions and to think of any remedial action for such distractions by way of certain disciplines and practices. There remains no one to think or feel or react to events. All that happens through that body-mind apparatus is seen as part of the functioning of Totality in the present moment. In other words, when apperception has happened, there does not exist any colloquial difference between the Reality that is, and the world of appearance, the relative reality that exists. The "difference", the boundary, the separation has also disappeared with the disappearance of the "me"-concept. Such intellectual dualism disappears with the apperception which is really the unity of vision: the manifest and the unmanifest, *samsara* and *nirvana*, are the One.

Ashtavakra continues:

"Impelled by the forces of causation in the evolutionary process, the body-mind organism of the desireless, independent being, free from all bondage, moves about in life like a dry leave in the breeze." (197)

"There is neither joy nor sorrow for him who has transcended worldly existence. Ever with a serene mind, he lives in the world as if without a body." (198)

"The steady one, abiding in the Self, with a mind that is calm and pure, finds nothing to renounce and is not concerned with losing anything anywhere." (199)

"With a mind that is vacant, living naturally and spontaneously, accepting life as it comes, the steady one, unlike the ordinary person, is not concerned with the concept of honor and dishonor." (200)

"The one who firmly believes that all actions which take place through the body-mind organism are not individual actions, does not act even though he appears to be acting." (201)

"The enlightened one lives naturally and spontaneously, and therefore his actions are not motivated by self-interest, but such actions for that reason are not those of a fool. For him, being in this world is like not being in this world. He is ever serene and contented." (202)

"The steady one, not interested in contentious reasoning and mentation, is free from conceptualization and is therefore always in repose. He has transcended thinking, knowing, hearing, and perceiving. (203)

"The wise one is not agitated or distracted in mind and thus sees no need for sitting in meditation. The question of bondage or freedom is irrelevant to him. In the full conviction that the apparent manifested universe is a figment of the imagination, he exists as the Consciousness itself." (204)

"The identified individual with a sense of volition acts even if he is not acting. On the other hand, the enlightened being, without any sense of personal doership, does not act even if there is action." (205)

"The mind of the enlightened one is neither agitated nor ecstatic. It is actionless, free from fluctuations, without desires. It shines, not being blocked by any doubts." (206)

"The mind of the enlightened one does not engage itself in either mentation or activity. If mentation or activity does take place, it is not out of a sense of volition or personal doership, but is natural and spontaneous." (207)

"Having heard the Truth, the dull-witted person becomes even more confounded, while an extremely intelligent man withdraws within himself to such an extent that he appears to others as being dull-witted." (208)

It needs a certain amount of spiritual evolution to be ready to receive the Truth when it is offered, to perceive the Truth when it is pointed out. As many a Master has said, when he was earnestly requested for enlightenment, "I am always ready to give you enlightenment, but are you prepared to accept it?"

The Kenopanishad brings out the fact that the knowledge of non-duality cannot be acceptable to all, that yonly be a certain type of intelligence. (It is a well-known fact that the principles of sub-atomic physics, which young doctorate students grasp quite quickly, are found to elude physicists who have been too well-grounded in Newtonian physics). It says, "The Self-existent God (Consciousness-in-action) has so created the senses that they tend to move outward, so that the human being perceives the external objective expression and not the subjective unmanifest within. Only perchance, a rare one, destined for enlightenment, turns his gaze inward and perceives the inner *Atman*." Then again, in the *Bhagavad Gita*, Lord Krishna says, "One perchance in thousands, seeks perfection; and one perchance among these blessed seekers finds Me in Reality."

> *"The confused and ignorant people are found to be continually involved in practices of mental concentration or in efforts to control the mind. The wise ones, on the other hand, like persons in deep sleep, do not see any necessity of doing anything."*
> *(209)*

In these verses, Ashtavakra describes various aspects of the non-volitional, spontaneous living of the sage after enlightenment has taken place. The simile of the dry leaf moving wherever the breeze takes it is a vivid example of the life style of the enlightened being. He lives without any personal effort and without any personal aim. Indeed it is the aimless flight of a dry leaf which was supposed to have been the immediate, apparent cause of illumination (sudden transformation), taking place in the case of Lao Tzu, when he sat under a tree, totally frustrated by the futility of all his efforts to see his real nature. It then suddenly struck him with a tremendous force that the very effort, the very desire to see into one's own nature is the obstruction to enlightenment.

In a similar strain, Omar Khayyam describes the living of a human being:

> *"The Ball no question makes*
> *of Ayes and Noes,*
> *But Here or There, as strikes*
> *the Player, goes;*
> *And He that tossed you*
> *down into the Field,*

He knows about it all—He
knows—HE knows!"

Ashtavakra describes the enlightened being as *nirvasanah, niralanbah*: one, whose desires have fallen off, and at the same time who has no need of crutches of any kind. The enlightened being without any desires, does not need any support, any conceptual crutch to lean on. It is for this reason that the sage further describes him as free and independent. He is totally "naked" as Jesus Christ wants the seeker to be. He is totally "poor" as Meister Eckhart describes the true seeker worthy of awakening. If you feel the need of a conceptual crutch to support your needs, you are not naked, nor poor. In any case, says Omar Khayyam, all your appeals will have been addressed only to a conceptual saviour:

"And that inverted Bowl
they call the Sky,
Whereunder crawling coop'd
we live and die,
Lift not your hands to It
for help -for It
As impotently moves as
You or I"

The very asking for help, for support in phenomenal life is done by an individual wanting his desires to be satisfied. Enlightenment means the erasing of all desire, of all expectation, but it does not mean any deliberate giving up of anything. Absence of desire means freedom from desire to want something that is not there as well as from the desire to give up deliberately something that is there. This is an important point that is often missed and therefore leads to considerable misunderstanding and confusion. Ashtavakra repeatedly expresses that the sage is totally unconcerned with both activity and inactivity, possession and renunciation. Indeed the sage is free from all pairs of opposites.

For "free" or "independent", Ashtavakra uses the word *"Swachhandah."* The colloquial meaning of the word is "willful" or "wayward" or "irresponsible." But the root meaning of the word is "being totally one with the inner Self", one who has become enamored with the song within, one who is united with the inner universal pulse. Such a one will be immune to the buffeting of the "sea of *samsara*" without.

Finally, in the verse describing the life of an enlightened being as the flight of a dry leaf in the breeze, the sage uses the words "free from bondage." Freedom from bondage of what? What is it that creates bondage? What creates bondage is conceptualizing, the creating of images, including that of Reality. Reality, as such, is a concept—let there be no doubt about this—and therefore unreal. And seeking such conceptual reality is itself bondage. It is such seeking which leads to the void of reality, but, indeed, the Void that is Reality is That which is devoid of the concept of reality. This means negating the negator who has negated the concept of phenomenality into a concept of the void of reality! The only way out of this bondage is by apperceiving that, as Hui Neng has said, "From the beginning nothing is—nothing is, no thing is, no object whatever, not even ourselves (as objects)." To put it another way, the "enlightened being" has not seen "his" Self-nature for the simple reason that It cannot be an object of a subject, and certainly not "his."

In the ultimate understanding, freedom from bondage means freedom from dualistic thinking. It is freedom from considering *nirvana* and *samsara* to exist, and to exist separately. Both *nirvana* and *samsara* are each a mode of perception, neither is an object or a thing. As conceptual objects, they can never be united, as Subjectivity, they can never be divided. Freedom from bondage means a sudden, instantaneous, subjective intuition of the unity of subject-and-object.

So, Ashtavakra says that the sage lives his life, wherever he is—whether among other people or in lonely places, wherever life has placed him—allowing himself to be tossed about, like a dry leaf, by the breeze of life. He accepts life as it comes, doing whatever has to be done without considering it as "his" doing. This "doing" will naturally include whatever thinking and planning might be necessary "Non-volitional living" has been misunderstood to an astonishing degree. It has been generally taken to mean the living of an idiot, but actually it is far from it. The sage makes it clear that the enlightened one lives naturally and spontaneously and his actions are not motivated by self-interest. Such actions for that reason are not those of a fool. Indeed, he goes further and says, "Having heard the Truth, the confused (dull-witted) person becomes even more confounded while an extremely intelligent man (on hearing the same) withdraws within himself to such an extent that he appears to others as being dull-witted." He appears to others as being dull-witted because he lives non-volitionally. He acts without any specific motive or aim. While living non-volitionally, while accepting life as it comes along, he is seen to be generally serene and unexcited, which to the average person means being dull-witted! The sage appears to be dull-witted to the average person because he seems (and is) indifferent to both praise and criticism.

Non-volitional living does not mean not taking medicines when unwell, nor does it mean deliberately not taking evasive steps to avoid an impending danger. To deliberately not do something or to deliberately give up something—is basically an act (a negative act) of volition. It is no different from the positive act of doing something. The whole point of non-volitional living is living without a sense of personal doership. This means merely witnessing whatever happens through all bodymind organisms, including "your" own, without comparing, without judging. Non-volitional living means neither deliberately sitting in meditation (with a conscious or unconscious motive and objective) nor deliberately avoiding meditation because of an inadequate understanding. Both are acts of volition. When the mind is quiet and falls into meditation, any attempt at resisting it is an act of volition, an act of violence. If meditation happens, welcome it, enjoy it. If meditation does not happen, do not hanker after it. This is the attitude of the sage after apperception has occurred.

Ashtavakra describes the sage as one who is not agitated or distracted in mind (because the split-mind has already been healed into its wholeness) and thus feels no need to sit in meditation. He further adds that he is not interested in the question of bondage and liberation: he is neither a *mumukshu* (seeker) nor anything else. In the full conviction that the apparent manifested universe is a figment in the imagination (an appearance in Consciousness) he exists as the *Brahman* itself. The meaning of *mumukshu* is "one who desires to achieve *moksha*, enlightenment." The generally accepted notion is that to be an earnest seeker, an ardent desire for enlightenment is a necessary condition. Of course, this has relevance only to the circumstance when the Self-enquiry (the question regarding God or divinity) is not really serious but merely a superficial matter. What Ashtavakra implies in this verse is that any desire, even the desire for *moksha* (enlightenment) is a serious obstacle in the way of the *happening* of enlightenment.

As the eleventh century Chinese sage Tsung Kao has put it, "If we want to grasp it, it runs away from us, but if we cast it away it continues to be there all the time."

What this clearly means is—and this is precisely what

Ashtavakra wants to point out—that we cannot make of enlightenment an object because That is our real nature. Or more accurately, That is What-We-Are. What Ashtavakra dares to point out (and it is for this reason that his work has not gained the popularity that other inferior works have) is that the ordinary mind and the enlightened mind are both illusions. All there is, is Consciousness (whole-mind). "It" or "That" is pure subjectivity without the slightest touch of objectivity; void, silence, purity, omnipresence. As a phenomenal object, the human being can never *"know"* it. We can only *become* this "mysterious peaceful joy" that is the non-volitional living of the sage.

What Ashtavakra dares to point out is that it is almost impossible to speak of enlightenment without talking nonsense. It is not an object to be attained by another object that is the human being. All that can happen is an awakening. The sage who has awakened from the living dream will have a recollection of the living dream just as a human being, after waking up in the morning, may have a recollection of the dream he dreamt in the night. The basic understanding that Ashtavakra proposes is that we *are* only in phenomenal dualistic manifestation. We are only in the living dream. Other than in duality, we cannot *be*. Thus, the need of reality, and the desire for enlightenment can only be figments of the imagination like the entire manifestation. In other words, the desire for reality is ridiculous not so much because there is no such thing but more because there is really no "one" to know whether or not there is anything. And when this very understanding brings about the ceasing of seeking both "outward" and "inward", it is, *phenomenally speaking*, "universal benediction" or *Sat-chit-ananda*.

The dual basis of all desire—whether the desire is for material welfare or spiritual welfare—is the ego (the "me"-concept) functioning in tandem with another concept, that of time (duration). Ashtavakra, therefore, says that the identified individual with a sense of volition acts even when he is not acting, whilst the enlightened being, not being burdened with a sense of doership, does not act even when there is action. It is generally believed that there cannot be any action without a sense of purpose, without a sense of doership, and that any teaching that precludes personal doership with a sense of personal responsibility will lead to laziness and inaction. What is not understood in taking this attitude is that it is impossible not to do anything. Even if no work is done manually, the mind will not cease its conceptualizing. This is the action the sage refers to when he says that the identified person with a sense of separate entity acts even when he appears not to be acting. In regard to the non-action of the sage, in which action takes place without any personal motivation, there is the incident where Ramana Maharshi, the sage of Arunachala, gave a practical demonstration without uttering a single word. When the Maharshi was walking up the hill with a group of followers, two people were discussing this very issue. After a short while, the Maharshi sat down on a rock for a little rest. He picked up a stick of wood lying nearby, borrowed a knife from one of them, and very neatly carved out a walking stick. He himself had a walking stick and did not need another. So he just left the new walking stick resting against the rock, and proceeded with the walk. Everyone understood the point of the silent demonstration.

A seeker of enlightenment sits in meditation and believes he is not doing anything. Yet his mind continues to create images. One of the first of these is that of himself working towards a great spiritual goal while hundreds and thousands of misguided souls are crazily engaged in amassing wealth and fame. The enlightened sage keeps doing whatever seems necessary in the circumstances without any sense of doership, and when the work has ceased, he sits quietly, his body and mind relaxed, his eyes closed—meditation happens. The seeker who sits in meditation with the intention of achieving enlightenment sits and waits impatiently for enlightenment to happen. When nothing happens, be becomes frustrated. He goes seeking some other teacher and some other path. He cannot help it. All this is part of an evolutionary process which will go on through many lives and many body-mind organisms. The process continues until a particular body-mind organism becomes evolved highly enough spiritually to receive the sudden apperception that the seeker cannot achieve what he is seeking because he is himself what he is seeking. The seeker is the *sought*. Until the evolution is complete, as Ashtavakra says, Truth only confounds the already confused seeker (though this is the process of spiritual evolution). However, the extremely intelligent person, one who is ready for the happening of sudden illumination, will accept the ineluctable fact that the illusory human individual cannot possibly have any volition or choice, and leave the entire matter of bondage and liberation to His will. And such surrender brings about a tremendous sense of freedom.

Ashtavakra proceeds with his teaching:

"Neither by action nor by inaction does an ignorant person attain tranquility; the wise one becomes tranquil merely by understanding what tranquility is." (210)

"In this world those who devote themselves to diverse practices do not come to realize their true nature, which is purity, intelligence, love, perfection, transcendent and free from any taint of objectivity." (211)

"The ignorant person does not attain liberation in spite of various disciplines and methods for controlling the mind. The blessed one stands established in the Self merely through intuitive

understanding." *(212)*

"*The ignorant person does not attain the Brahman that he desires whereas the wise one realizes the nature of the Supreme Brahman even without desiring to do so.*" *(213)*

"*Without the necessary support, ignorant people keep seeking the illusion of enlightenment and thus feed the illusion of the manifested universe of* samsara. *The wise strike at the very root of the problem.*" *(214)*

"*The fool tries to attain tranquility through personal effort and fails to get it. The wise one apperceives the Truth directly and is ever tranquil.*" *(215)*

One rarely comes across Truth put so succinctly and so powerfully as when Ashtavakra declares, "Neither by action nor by inaction does an ignorant person attain tranquility; the wise one becomes tranquil merely by understanding what tranquility is." Tranquility means acceptance of What-Is, without wanting to change it. It means acceptance of what one is without wanting to become something else. The basis of acceptance is living in the present moment, accepting the present experience with the full understanding that it must change because change is the very essence of phenomenal life and living.

It is accepting the present experience totally and completely, neither wanting to hang on to it because it is acceptable, nor wanting to move away from it because it is unacceptable. Happiness has come to mean an imagined situation where health and pleasure abound to the exclusion of sickness, pain and suffering. The pursuit of such illusory happiness results in boredom, a sense that life is meaningless, frustration and fear in the midst of apparent plenty. Tranquility, on the other hand, means the absence of resistance to the experience of the present moment. And it is understanding this with total conviction which makes the wise man tranquil all the time. Ashtavakra, in other words, says that tranquility cannot be achieved by either action or inaction; it can come about only by understanding very clearly what prevents tranquility from happening.

Ashtavakra uses the word *"moodha"* for the fool and the ignorant person. He does not mean by that word one who is an ignoramus. Indeed, the *"moodha"* can be a very learned man, but his perception, his perspective is incorrect. He looks in the wrong direction. The *moodha*, believing himself a separate individual doer, perceives the outside through his senses and interprets what he perceives according to personal criteria. Such perceiving is done by the split-mind perceiving the phenomenal objects as its objects, and is thus the foolish perceiving of the *moodha*. The wise man, on the other hand, sees the Truth as the sudden perceiving of subject and object as one. The wise man's perceiving is a sudden flood-light, an intuitive perceiving of the unity of subject and object. It is whole-mind perceiving. The *moodha* gives importance to the thoughts which arise in the split-mind and ignores the intervals between thoughts. The wise man merely witnesses the thoughts which arise and realizes that the intervals between thoughts are truly What-WeAre—Consciousness not intruded upon by mentation. Thoughts arising in the split-mind or conditioned personal consciousness are concerned with the identified dream figure in this living dream. The intervals between thoughts provide in-tuition—the looking within - which is our real, impersonal "Self." So, when Ashtavakra uses the word *"moodha"*, he means not necessarily an unlearned man or an idiot. He is referring to one who does not yet possess the intuitive receptivity of the "blessed" one who, like Nisargadatta Maharaj, may be only barely literate. It is said that Hui Neng, an illiterate Chinese peasant, suddenly had a flash of intuitive understanding when he heard a *sutra* being recited while he was walking along the road, and ultimately became the sixth Patriarch. The monk, who was probably reciting the sutra for the umpteenth time, was certainly not an unlearned man but was, according to Ashtavakra, a *moodha* if he had not apperceived the Truth being announced in the *sutra*.

Ashtavakra proceeds to say quite explicitly that those who devote themselves to diverse practices and disciplines do not come to realize their true nature. In the absence of intuitive understanding—the necessary support—the *moodha* keeps seeking an illusory object called enlightenment and in the process, gets more and more befuddled in the illusion of *samsara*.

As Ramana Maharshi said:

"Do not meditate—Be!"
Do not think that you are—Be!
Do not think about being—you Are!"

The Maharshi was quite clear that in the beginning, when the urge had just turned the mind inward, regular times of formal practice and discipline were good. But he did not recommend long periods of sitting in meditation. As the understanding begins to dawn, if the practices and disciplines are not persisted with stubbornly, a sense of deeper beatitude will arise spontaneously without the intrusion of the "me"-concept. While ones hands are busy at work, ones head will be cool in silence and solitude. The Maharshi invariably showed his disapproval whenever any of the devotees showed an inclination, or asked for permission to give up their usual mundane activities in order to take up a meditative life.

Ramana Maharshi was equally emphatic against any practices to control the mind. He would say, "Show me the mind and I shall tell you what to do with it." He would assert that the mind, being merely a collection of thoughts, cannot be extinguished by another thought, desire or decision. The mind (the ego, the "me"-concept) is only fattened by such new thoughts. As Ashtavakra says, the ignorant people (*moodha*) by their seeking only feed the illusion of *samsara*.

The fact of the matter is that "enlightenment" is phenomenally a subjective state: how can that subjective state be affected by a manifested appearance? A shadow cannot either know or affect its substance, an appearance cannot either know or affect its source. All there is, is Consciousness. Who then practices? Who seeks what? Obviously, it can only be Consciousness itself that seeks. And what does it seek? Itself, of course. The entire manifestation is an impersonal process which science today calls "a self-generated process." Consciousness first creates an appearance within itself. This is followed by Consciousness identifying itself with each individual manifested object. Consciousness thus personifies its impersonality and creates the further illusion of the individual ego within the general illusion of manifestation. Finally, it starts the process of disidentification—receding from the personal to the impersonal which ends in the phenomenal occurrence known as awakening, or illumination or enlightenment.

Why all this?

Why not?

It is all Consciousness or God in a divine play. The potential primal energy actuates itself as manifested objects and then merges back within itself in due course. The entire process is of the nature of a dream, an illusion. And in this impersonal process, the supposed individual is really quite irrelevant (as the cause). This is the intuitive understanding which brings about the "awakening." And it is precisely the absence of this in-tuition (in-sight), which produces efforts and disciplines which "fatten the illusion of the manifested *samsara*." In other words, those who are still seeking are still self-anchored identities, and it is practically impossible for identities to find their own absence, which is what enlightenment is all about.

To put this differently, enlightenment is the *normal* Noumenal condition of our beingness. The absence of enlightenment is the *current* condition wherein Consciousness has identified itself with each phenomenal object. "Enlightenment" means recovery from the *current* condition to the *normal* condition. It means receding from the current illusion of personal autonomy into the original normal condition of universal impersonal beingness. It is unfortunate, but perhaps unavoidable, that the very term "enlightenment" or "liberation" is the cause of the entire confusion since it inevitably has the implication that there is "someone" to be enlightened. And yet such understanding is comported in the final, ultimate understanding that there is truly nothing to be understood by any "one."

Ashtavakra therefore exhorts the disciple to believe that never will the misguided individual ever attain enlightenment by any kind of disciplines, any kind of practices, any kind of sacrifices. He asserts that the bondage itself is an illusion and the only way out of this bondage of misunderstanding is through the understanding—that from the beginning nothing is, other than Consciousness. There is no thing, no object whatever, not even the human being. The human being is really not an individual object but the impersonal sense of presence, Consciousness, here and now, changeless and immutable, ever present, which does not need to be realized. The only thing to be "done" is to be as we are. The only thing to be surrendered is the idea that we have autonomy and independence of choice and action. The misunderstanding is that one wants to *become*

Consciousness, the beginning of understanding is "*I am Consciousness*" the ultimate understanding is "All there is, is Consciousness."

> "*How can there be any seeing of Self-nature for one who sees only this object or that object when he perceives the phenomenal manifestation? The wise, when they see the manifestation, perceive not this object or that object, but only Consciousness in which it has appeared.*" (216)

> "*How can the deluded one, who strives for it, control the mind? For the wise one who is established in the Self, the whole-mind needs no control in its spontaneity.*" (217)

> "*There are some who believe in the existence of the phenomenal manifestation, and there are others who believe that phenomenal manifestation does not exist. Rare is the one who is not concerned with such concepts, and is therefore always serene.*" (218)

> "*Those with an immature intellect may believe that the Atman is pure and without a second, yet they want to experience the Atman phenomenally as an independent entity. Therefore, they continue to be unhappy as long as they live.*" (219)

> "*The intellect of the seeker seeking enlightenment cannot function without a corresponding object as its support. The intellect of the liberated person is not limited and restricted by any desire even for liberation.*" (220)

In this set of verses, Ashtavakra again emphasizes the basic point that phenomenally all are objects, some sentient and others insentient, some animate and others inanimate. Therefore there cannot be a *phenomenal* subject perceiving an object as his object. But this is precisely what the fool does and what the wise man does not do. In other words, the "bondage" consists in believing that there exists an independent, autonomous entity as an observer as *opposed to* that which is observed. The wise man, with an intuitive understanding of the basic unity in all objects which constitute the totality of manifestation, realizes that all perceiving is a subjective or Noumenal functioning. Phenomenally *there cannot be a phenomenal subject* perceiving anything as his object.

Therefore it can only be Consciousness which does the perceiving (in its aspect as sentience, through the instrumentation of the senses in a sentient object) of everything that is manifested as its own objective expression, within itself. This is the understanding of the wise man. It is an understanding in which there does not exist any individual comprehender as an entity. This is what the sage means when he says that the wise, when they see the manifestation, perceive not this object or that object (separate from themselves, as *their* objects) but only Consciousness in which the manifestation has appeared.

The sage says that the bondage of the deluded person lies only in the fact that he does not consider himself as the object that he actually is (like any other object in manifestation) but as the subject of the objects he thinks *he* perceives. In other words, bondage is the usurpation of subjectivity by a sentient object. The human sentient object mistakenly believes that he is the subject whereas what he really is, is not the subject but the sentience *within*. Yet sometimes such a misunderstanding does not totally eclipse the intuitive in-seeing and thus begins the seeking of the seeker for his real nature. The joke, of course, is that the seeker still thinks in terms of himself as an individual subjective entity and seeks his real nature (enlightenment) as an object! It is for this reason that every Master of *Advaita* (non-duality) keeps reiterating that enlightenment means nothing other than the realization that enlightenment is not some thing to be attained. Nor is it some thing not to be attained. It is not that we already possess it (as is sometimes mistakenly stated), but for the simpler reason that enlightenment is What We-Are (not what we *think* we are). *This* which is seeking is as illusory as *that* which is sought. It is for this reason that the Buddha was compelled to say that he had *attained* nothing whatsoever.

As phenomenal objects we can never *know* That. Nor can we *become* That because we *are* That. And in this understanding, in this apperception, all thinking, all seeking, all reaching ceases. The sage asks, how can there be any seeing of one's Self-nature by one who sees only this object or that object when he perceives the phenomenal manifestation? Apperception can never happen so long as there is perceiving of something as a separate object. Such perceiving is inevitably accompanied by a psychic interpretation of that perception as acceptable or unacceptable.

There is a story about the female Sufi, Fakir Raabia. She was sitting inside her hut one early morning, abiding in the Self, immersed in meditation. Another Fakir by the name of Hassan was passing by on his way to the mosque. It was a lovely morning, and Hassan was enjoying the cool breeze around him, the last of the stars in the early morning sky. He noticed that Raabia had not come out of the hut, and so he called out to her, "Raabia, what are you doing in there, when the Almighty is creating for us such a lovely morning which even the birds are enjoying freely and expressing their delight in song. Why not come out and appreciate this beauty of the Almighty's universe?" Raabia laughed and answered,

"Hassan, my friend, how long will you stay out and see the beauty outside? Come within and know That which has created this beauty outside." And instantly, Hassan realized the depth of understanding that Raabia had reached. He realized that looking outside, one will see only objects. Looking within, it must be clearly understood, you will not see the subject, because if you did, the subject you see will only be another object. If you see your face in the mirror, you will see your image. Even if you remove the mirror and keep your eyes closed, in your split-mind's eye, you will still see the image of your face. Truly seeing within, you will see not yourself as the subject because there can be no subject phenomenally. What you will perhaps see is the absence of yourself as an object. This absence is often described as the "void." So long as an object in his mistaken identity as the subject, sees another object, there can never be the realization that all objects are the objectivization, the mirrorization of subjectivity. Such a realization is the void of apperception in which the unity of object and subject is perceived. And, most important, even this void is a concept. The ultimate realization happens only when the negator of this negation is himself negated. That is to say, when the seeking itself ceases.

Ashtavakra continues to describe the spontaneous, non-volitional living of the awakened being:

"Encountering the tigers of sense-objects, the frightened seeker takes refuge in the cave of the mind, and tries various methods of disciplining and controlling the mind." (221)

"Encountering the desireless lion-hearted being, the elephants of sense-objects either quietly slip away, or otherwise, are totally subservient like servile courtiers." (222)

"He whose Self-realization is totally without any doubts at all finds no need to resort to any disciplinary practices as a means to liberation. Seeing, hearing, touching, smelling and tasting, he lives happily." (223)

"With the split-mind healed into its holy wholeness by the mere listening to the Truth, and with total serenity prevailing continually, he is not concerned with the propriety or otherwise of any action, nor with inaction." (224)

"Free from a sense of doership, the wise person does whatever needs to be done in the circumstances, without concerning himself with the propriety of the action; his actions are like the actions of a child." (225)

"Through freedom, comes happiness; through freedom, the best; through freedom, tranquility; through freedom is attained the Supreme State." (226)

In regard to sense-experiences, attitude makes all the difference between the ordinary person and the Self-realized one. As Saint Jnaneshwar puts it, "The *sevanti* flower (spreading flower) expands into a thousand petals but it spreads within itself. Similarly, even when new and fresh experiences are noticed in the life of a Self-realized person, they are not experienced by him as volitional experiences since his living is entirely non-volitional." The ignorant person reacts to all events by interpreting them as pleasant or unpleasant and strives in future to have fresh experiences which he considers pleasant and to avoid the unpleasant ones. The Self-realized person, on the other hand, lives spontaneously and naturally, having realized the nature of all events as mere movements in Consciousness. His living is always in the present moment, he accepts events as they occur, without any psychic interpretation as acceptable or unacceptable.

Therefore, says Saint Jnaneshwar, senses according to their nature may run towards objects which are supposed to satisfy them, but almost simultaneously there is the instant realization that the experience is not different from what he himself (the Self-realized) is. It is as when the sight meets the mirror and there is the instant realization that the image in the mirror is not different from the face. An experience is generally regarded as an event, but in fact an experience has no existence in itself. An experience is merely the effect of reacting to an outside impulse or stimulus and such reaction is then recorded in memory as pleasant or unpleasant for future reference. In other words, *an experience is never factual, only conceptual.* The point is that it is always a "me" (an object), who has an experience. The same event may produce different reactions, different experiences, in different psychosomatic organisms, each considering itself a separate entity with a name. The body-mind organisms are actually mere instruments or characters through which Totality provides events that are termed life and living. The reactions to these events, because of identification with the body, are what cause the supposed "bondage." Since the reactions are merely conceptual, the bondage must obviously be conceptual too.

In other words, That-which-we-are is subjective without the slightest touch of objectivity, and it is the objective which suffers an experience. Identifying with this (body) which has an experience is what the ordinary person does. *Being the experience* is what happens after enlightenment or Self-realization. The experiencing of pleasure or pain is part of the total functioning, and therefore, impersonal and non-objective. It is only when the experiencing is interpreted (through the dualistic process of subject-object relationship) as an experiencer experiencing an experience in the duration of time sequence that the experiencing loses its impersonal, intemporal element and becomes an individual, personal experience.

Saint Jnaneshwar illustrates this point with some good examples. He says, for instance, that if you tried to lift up a wave, all you will lift is water. Also, three different kinds of gold ornaments may have three different shapes and three different names, but all three of them are basically gold. You will have three different sensorial experiences of touch, sight and taste but the object will still be camphor. Similarly, says Jnaneshwar, whatever the experiences, all of them can happen only in Consciousness. Thus, as soon as the senses like seeing, hearing, touching, smelling and tasting go forward to meet their respective objects, the experience in the Selfrealized state, is realized for what it is—a manifestation in Consciousness, a modification of the mind—and therefore a subject-object relationship is not established.

This absence of subject-object relationship is illustrated by the instance when Hui Neng, the illiterate peasant who later became the Sixth Patriarch, pointed out to two monks who were arguing about the flapping of the flag, that the flapping was actually neither the wind nor the flag itself but the mind that observed them.

Though the wind was the apparent or immediate cause, the ultimate or basic cause was mind or Consciousness. All phenomena, all events have an apparent or immediate cause, but both the event and the cause are phenomenal appearances. The basic or ultimate cause is always necessarily Consciousness. In the absence of Consciousness, there would be no cognizing. The apparent cause may be understood, along with its effect, as being horizontal (in duration) or phenomenal, while the basic cause is always vertical (outside duration) or Noumenal. The basic cause is never the positive or the negative phenomenal appearance, never the immediate cause and effect, dualistic subject and object. It is always Consciousness, which is all there is, ever was or ever will be.

"As the understanding deepens, the outward tendencies of the mind get weakened with the realization that the Self within is neither the doer nor the experiencer." (227)

"The non-volitional, spontaneous, unrestricted behavior o f the wise man is transparently open and sincere but not the affected tranquility exhibited by the one who is still governed by personal motives and considerations." (228)

"The steady ones, totally free from all conceptualizing, and bereft of all attachments are sometimes found in affluent surroundings, and at other times in mountain-caves." (229)

"There is total detachment in the heart of the steady one in whatever circumstances he finds himself, in whatever company—a vedic scholar being honored or the gods being worshipped, or in a holy place or in the company of a king or a woman or a loved one." (230)

"The yogi is not disturbed even when despised or ridiculed by servants, sons, wives, grandsons, and other relations." (231)

"Though pleased, he is not pleased; though dejected, he is not dejected. Only those who are themselves

like him will understand this wonderful state of beingness." (232)

"The sense of duty, pertinent only to samsara, *is transcended by the wise ones who have realized their true nature as all-pervasive, formless, immutable, untainted." (233)*

The outward tendencies of the mind can neither be controlled by psycho-physical practices and disciplines (except temporarily, and even then they become addictions) nor can they be got rid of (except temporarily) through escapes like alcohol and drugs which ultimately end in disaster. All escapes, including television and other forms of entertainment, are merely an effort to get away from the identification of the "me" as the doer and the experiencer. Change of environment may produce a certain kind of temporary relaxation for the body and mind, but greed and envy will continue to rear their heads in any environment and any circumstances. In watching a movie, for instance, the purpose is to forget oneself, but all that happens is that the "me" gets identified with a character in the movie, and suffers his experiences, pleasures and miseries. Dis-identification is the only answer, and this, says the sage, can only happen when there is a deep understanding that this life and living is only a great dream in which all human beings are thrown in as characters. It is only the Self, the impersonal dreamer witnessing the dream, who transcends the doing and the experiencing in the dream. The dreamed character can do nothing about the events in the dream. You identify yourself with the dreamed character as the doer and the experience, and you suffer the consequences of the doing, which is the experiencing. You disidentify yourself from the dreamed character and you instantly become the Self, the Subject. You are the dreamer merely witnessing the objective manifestation, so long as the dreamed manifestation exists. Once the objective manifestation is seen with deep conviction as not being separate from the Subjective Self (the formless unmanifest), the "one" or the "me" no longer exists with a split-mind of subject-object with "outward tendencies."

Such an understanding with deep conviction, a sudden instantaneous subjective intuition of the unity between the unmanifest and the manifest, is what the Chinese sage Huang Po meant when he said that it is only in the sudden perceiving of subject-and-object-as-one that the truth is revealed. And this unity, says another Chinese sage, is the absence of the absence of both subject and object as *phenomena*, a voidness or no-thing-ness in which there is inevitable indivisible *Unicity*.

What Ashtavakra says here is that positive disciplines and practices by a "me" as the doer are not going to bring about the annihilation of the "me"-concept as a doer and experiencer. It is only the deepest possible belief—which itself cannot be acquired!—that volition for the human being is an illusion that will lead to an acceptance of His will in all that happens. Then the feeling of doing and experiencing will be replaced by the sense of merely witnessing events impersonally. Events will no longer be interpreted as acceptable or unacceptable. And such absence of interpretation will inevitably mean absence of experiencing the interconnected phenomena of alternating pleasure and pain as the experiencer. It must, of course, be understood very clearly, throughout this great teaching, that words alone can never transfer the required understanding. They can only open the way for the pre-existing intuition to rise into Consciousness. In other words, what is generally understood as understanding is only intellectual comprehension. This the Master seeks to reveal, so that (at the appropriate time, when Grace occurs) when the turning-over of the mind occurs as a self-generated process, there will be an instant recognition of the absence of oneself as an individual entity.

It is part of the cosmic joke that, even having intellectually understood that objective understanding is by itself not only futile but could actually be a hindrance, you cannot stop seeking such objective understanding.

The spontaneous urge which turned you into a seeker in the first place will not let you stop seeking. Yet this is necessary, because it is only the deepest frustration generated by the objective comprehender which will be the catalyst, at the appropriate time (over which you can have no control), for that very objective comprehension to be suddenly transformed into subjective apperception. As Ma Tzu, the Chinese Master put it, "In the Tao there is nothing to discipline oneself in. If there is any discipline in it, the completion of such discipline means the destruction of the Tao. But if there is no discipline whatever in the Tao, one remains an ignoramus."

The subjective apperception of Truth automatically leads to the spontaneous, non-volitional, natural behavior of the *jnani*. It is behavior that is obviously sincere because he is not concerned with what others may think of him. Indeed he does not consider it as "his" behavior. He merely witnesses all "his" actions as part of the functioning of Totality through a particular body-mind apparatus. Ashtavakra says the sage's behavior is unrestricted. This simply means that the sage is not necessarily the model of exemplary behavior. His behavior is perfectly natural in the circumstances, not necessarily "gentlemanly" except to the obvious extent that he will never *intentionally* be rude or angry or insulting, even though his behavior may be interpreted, or rather, misinterpreted, as such by others.

Saint Jnaneshwar, in his own inimitable way, emphasizes the fact that, in the case of the Self-realized (the *jnani*), you cannot have any relative criteria at all. He says: "Wherever the *jnani* places his foot is his pilgrimage, and if he does go on a pilgrimage it is as if he has not moved at all. It is no wonder, therefore, that for the *jnani-Bhakta*, it makes no difference whether he stays in one place or moves about from place to place, whether he is in the company of others or in solitude. Since the *jnani* sees no difference between the Noumenon and the phenomena, whatever he sees is the form of Shiva and thus he enjoys the privilege of having seen Shiva (the 'privilege' is only from the viewpoint of the ordinary individual). On the other hand, if he does see the form of Shiva (on a visit to the temple) it is not as if he has seen anything out of the ordinary because there is no difference between Shiva and the *jnani*."

The basic essential of the state of universal Consciousness (of the Self-realized *jnani*) as Ashtavakra says, can be known only by someone who is "himself" in that state. And that basic essential is not to move away, not to resist the experience of the present moment. Such resistance at once implies the existence of an individual experiencer judging the present experience as acceptable or unacceptable. He resists the experience if it is judged as unacceptable or he resists any change if it is judged as being acceptable. Such resistance—either to the present experience or to change—transforms the eternity of the present moment into the transience of the passing present as time or duration. What Ashtavakra says is that it is only someone living in the present moment of tranquility who will recognize another who is also living in the present moment, for the simple reason that there is neither the one nor the other, but only the eternal present moment witnessing the passing show of illusion. Being in the present moment, we are the Noumenal. Interpreting the present moment as acceptable or unacceptable, we project ourselves into the phenomenal, into time and duration, into fear and misery, hope and frustration, birth and death. Being in the eternal present moment means realizing the inescapable, fundamental unity between *nirvana* and *samsara*. Slipping away from the present moment into duration means floundering in the "sea of *samsara*." Regaining of the intuition—the inseeing—of the unity of *samsara* and *nirvana* means enlightenment, being in the eternal present moment. And, most importantly, being in the present moment, none of this has any relevance or importance!

The sage is in the present moment, not concerned with whatever *happens* in the duality of phenomenality. He is merely witnessing it. The matter of what should be done and what should not be done—the sense of duty and obligation—is of no relevance at ail to him who *knows* that he is not doing anything. The sage knows that all events happen through the instrumentation of various human beings, who were born with the natural characteristics, needed those particular events to happen.

Being in the present moment also comports an aspect of understanding that is not generally recognized. The present moment does exist in the spiritual evolution (in phenomenal duration) but only when it is not associated with the past or future. Then the present moment becomes the eternal present moment. Such disassociation with duration of past and future will bring about acceptance of whatever happens in each present moment.

All that one need "do" (so long as the transcendence of the "doer" has not taken place) is to cease having doubts whether one is on the right path or not. The location at any present moment for any individual in the spiritual evolution cannot but be right and proper. With this understanding all one can do is to concentrate on whatever one is doing without any doubts about it. *Whenever any change is needed, it will take place.* Accept that change when it takes place is His will, and you will continue to remain in the eternal present. And then suddenly it will happen—the intuition of subjectivity, the basis of which is the total absence of individual volition and choice, accompanied (phenomenally) by a sudden enormous feeling of total freedom, all doubts erased, all things settled, nothing but peace. And, of course, *all this can happen only if there is no barrier of expectation!*

Ashtavakra continues:

"One who is unstilled is always agitated through distraction even when doing nothing; the expert, even when he is busy working, remains totally imperturbable." (234)

"Even in everyday life, the wise one with equanimity is always happy, whether he is relaxing, sleeping, generally going about his business, speaking or eating." (235)

"He is the perfect model for living, who, having realized his true nature, unlike the ordinary individual, carries on in everyday life unruffled and unagitated like a vast lake." (236)

"With the deluded one, even withdrawal becomes action; in the case of the steady one, even continued action brings about the fruit of withdrawal." (237)

"The moodha is often seen to display indifference towards his possessions. Where is attachment or detachment for him who has lost identification with the body?" (238)

"The moodha is always busy conceptualizing; the one abiding in the present moment does think when thinking is necessary in what he is doing, and yet he is not thinking." (239)

This set of verses discusses a point about which there is a great deal of confusion and misunderstanding: what is "thinking." When Ramana Maharshi said, "Thinking is not man's real nature", he obviously did not mean that one should be like an idiot. What he obviously meant by "thinking" is "conceptualizing" or creating images in the mind, thinking other than that which is necessarily and immediately relevant to the doing. Thinking relevant to the doing becomes part of the doing, which is necessarily part of the functioning of Totality. Thinking—discriminating or judging between alternatives—as a mental process is an essential element of phenomenal life because the very basis of phenomenality is duality, the interconnectedness of opposites. Therefore, comparing and judging is a necessary part of living and cannot be avoided. But what can be avoided—and indeed is absent where there is enlightenment—is the sense of personal doership. In other words, when enlightenment has happened such discriminating as is necessary in life happens spontaneously as part of the functioning of Totality.

The whole problem of daily ordinary life is the fact that the individual firmly believes that it is he who is working. Where enlightenment has happened, the understanding has also been firmly established that the real source of all activity is Consciousness itself, the functioning of Totality. It is Consciousness which vivifies the mind and enables it to do all the work that is being done. In the case of the *jnani* there is no question of this fact being forgotten (which is the complaint of the average seeker) because the personal identity has been replaced by "Self-identity." It is for this reason too that there is no question of the mind of the Self-realized person, the *jnani*, being perturbed: he is not concerned with the success or failure of whatever is being done. In the words of Ramana Maharshi, "solitude is in the mind." One might be in the thick of the world and maintain serenity of mind. Such a one is in solitude. Another may stay in a forest, but still be unable to control his mind.

Such a man cannot be said to be in solitude. Solitude is a function of the mind. A man attached to desires cannot get solitude wherever he may be, whereas a detached man is always in solitude wherever he may be. Work performed with attachment is a shackle, whereas work performed with detachment does not affect the (apparent) doer. "One who works like this is in solitude, even while working. Solitude means tranquility, serenity, being at peace, unruffled.

There is a remarkable phrase in Zen Buddhism, "*honshomyoshu*", which is said to mean "instant awakening in wondrous practice." When there is sudden enlightenment, the usual question that follows an intellectual comprehension cannot arise: I have understood what you have said, but having understood that there is no individual do-er, how do I function in life—what do I do in everyday life? Sudden enlightenment is itself wondrous practice. It means simply witnessing whatever happens. It means a continuous living in the present moment as the joyous expression of the instant awakening. It means a healing of the split-mind of subject and object, between volition and non-volition, control and spontaneity. Once having accepted the self-generated spontaneity of the happening of events, an absence of volition and control is no longer a frightening matter. Spontaneity is no longer fearfully seen as chaos. Happiness then no longer seems something one has to make an effort to produce in duration. One is thus more easily able to enjoy and appreciate the simple joy of the present moment. One's sense of values changes and the effort towards more and more sophistication is seen as useless and futile. While the *moodha* (deluded ordinary individual) is unhappy chasing illusory happiness, the man of perfect understanding hears the source of constant joy, springing from within, in the eternal present moment.

Ashtavakra continues:

"*The man of solitude has no personal motive or*

aim in any undertaking that is started, lives with the innocence of a child, and has no attachment to the work that he produces." (240)

"Blessed is the man of understanding who has transcended the mind, who remains unmoved under all conditions while physically continuing to see, hear, touch, smell or taste." (241)

"For the man of perfection, changeless like space, how can there be any samsara or its manifestation? How can there be any end or the means to achieve it?" (242)

"Glorious is the beingness of one who, being free from all desires, is the embodiment of perfect bliss that is his real nature, and remains always spontaneously absorbed in pure Consciousness." (243)

"What is the use of saying anything more? The great soul who has had the perfect understanding is free from all desire, not only for sensual enjoyment but even for the enjoyment of enlightenment. He is totally devoid of all attachment, at all times, at all places." (244)

"What can remain to be done by one who is himself pure Consciousness? He has totally renounced the manifested world, the multiplicity of which exists only in different names, which begin with Mahat⁴." (245)

---

4 Cosmic intelligence

"The pure one knows with certitude that this universe is the product of illusion and that nothing really exists. The imperceptible Self has been revealed to him and he naturally enjoys the tranquility." (246)

"Rules of conduct, dispassion, renunciation and control over mind are all terms which arc meaningless to one who is of the nature of Pure Effulgence and who does not perceive any objective reality." (247)

"How can the terms bondage and liberation, joy and sorrow, have any meaning for one who shines as the Infinite, objectifying itself in endless forms, and does not recognize relative existence?" (248)

"With the happening of sudden enlightenment, the reality of the universe is seen as an illusion. The wise one lives totally devoid of any sense of "me" or "mine", and is therefore quite unattached to anything." (249)

"How can the wise one, who has apperceived the Self as imperishable and free from grief, who is without the feeling "I am the body" or "the body is mine", ever be interested in the universe or knowledge?" (250)

Ashtavakra says in the first verse in the series that the man of solitude (*muni*) has no personal motive when anything is undertaken. The word *muni* comes from the word *mouna*, meaning silence or mental solitude or equanimity or tranquility. An ordinary human being usually would not begin anything unless he has a motive, an end to fulfill, and the means with which to achieve that end. But for the *jnani* living his life spontaneously, having already lost his sense of personal doership, he has nothing to achieve and is therefore not concerned with the means either. When the ego (identification with a personal entity as a "me") goes, all personal sense of doership and achievement goes with it. Then all that happens through the body-mind organism is merely witnessed, without any comparison or judgement.

A wave in the ocean, if it were to animate and become infused with intellect, would at once begin to think in terms of a separate "me", and would instantly make itself unhappy by comparing itself with other waves. Once it identifies itself as a separate entity, it loses its identification with the ocean. By identifying yourself with a bodymind organism as a separate entity with a sense of doership, you lose your identity with Totality. How does it profit a man to gain the whole world and lose his own soul, his identity with Totality? You may gain the whole world yet it is still only an infinitesimal part of the enormous illusion of the universe, and in the process you lose your identity with Totality. And with the gain of the whole world comes the fear that you may lose it someday! The *muni*, on the other hand, having realized his true nature as Noumenon when unmanifest, and as the Totality when manifested, is totally dis-identified from the personal entity. Neither the end nor the means has any interest for him.

When the *muni* does explain the truth that the human being is merely an instrument through which Totality functions, and that the human organism (infused with breath and intellect) cannot possibly have any kind of volition, the *moodha* simply cannot accept it. "How can the world go on if each human being did not have ambition and work hard to achieve it?" he argues. "How can any work go on without personal motivation?" The *muni* will probably leave the matter at that, knowing that Truth cannot be accepted without the appropriate receptivity which itself is a matter of "Grace." Or perhaps he may relate the story of a rock lying in a pile: A child, going home from school at the end of the day, picked up the rock and with all the repressed energy threw it in the air. The rock was delighted and told his colleagues in the pile, "we all wished we could fly, but it is only me who can do it, and here I am in the air like a bird." It hit a window pane and the glass was shattered, and the rock said, "this is what happens when something gets in my way. I break it into small pieces. So beware." The rock fell on a mattress kept in the sun on the balcony, and it said, "I was obviously expected and my host has kept this soft mattress for me to rest on." Hearing the sound of broken glass, a servant came to the balcony, saw the stone and picked it up, and the rock thought, "here I am being welcomed like royalty." The servant threw the rock back into the pile, and the rock said to his colleagues, "1 was beginning to feel homesick, and here I am back home among you, after a wonderful experience." The child threw the rock because that was his nature, the rock came in contact with the glass and according to the inherent nature of each, the glass broke. The mattress happened to be where it was, and the servant threw the rock out, but the interpretation by the rock of a perfectly natural, spontaneous event was purely personal.

Breathing goes on by itself and the *moodha* thinks he is breathing. Thoughts come from outside—every fresh thought after a mental vacuum is a spontaneous event—and he thinks it is he who is thinking. Thoughts get transformed into action, and he thinks it is he who is acting! The *muni*, on the other hand, merely witnesses the event of seeing, hearing, touching, smelling or tasting as an event in which he is not concerned as an individual because the sense of personal doership has evaporated altogether.

It is an interesting point that in the *Bhagavad Gita*, Lord Krishna asks Arjuna to do his duty without expecting any results or the "fruits of the efforts." Ashtavakra goes to the root of the matter, and says that if there is no personal interest in starting an undertaking, the question of being interested in the fruits of the effort simply does not arise. To consider the effort and the undertaking as having been started by a "me" and then to expect the "me" not to be interested in the result is far more difficult than to understand deeply with conviction that the "me" is merely a conceptual creation. The "me" is quite incapable of "doing" anything except misconstruing as "his" doing, what is being done by Totality through a particular psychosomatic instrument, as "his" doing.

The *moodha* (the deluded one) is he who still has a sense of personal doership, but has the half-baked "knowledge" that he has no control over the results. So if the something "good" happens, he thanks the Lord, perhaps gives part of the profits in charity, all with the definite hope that the Lord will continue to shower His blessing on him. If something "bad" happens, he will undertake some disciplinary practices or do some *puja* or give something in charity in anticipation of not having any more failures. This is not *acceptance* of His will. Indeed in true acceptance, there is no acceptor at all. There is only acceptance, an impersonal apperception that the manifestation is a self-generated process. There is really no question of any "one" understanding anything or accepting anything. The ultimate understanding (apperception) can only be pure silence. In this silence the individual and his effort and the fruit of the effort all become irrelevant.

It is for this reason that the sage Ashtavakra keeps repeating that the pure one knows with certitude that this universe is the product of illusion and that from the beginning nothing is. There really has never been any beginning nor is there any end. The imperceptible Self has been revealed to him and he naturally enjoys tranquility in all circumstances. Ashtavakra adds that rules of conduct, dispassion, renunciation and control over mind are all terms which become meaningless as soon as there is a sudden apperception of the pure effulgence which is both the unmanifest and the manifest, both *samsara* and *nirvana*. Indeed in the void of apperception there is neither ignorance nor knowledge, neither bondage nor liberation. There is only an absolute absence of all concepts.

Ashtavakra says that with the happening of sudden enlightenment, the reality of the universe is seen only as an illusion. The wise one lives totally devoid of any sense of "me" and "mine", and is therefore quite unattached to anything. How can the wise one who has apperceived the Self as imperishable and free from grief, ever be interested in the universe or desire any knowledge about it? The apperception is transcendent, above thought and words (which are only vocalized thought). As one Chinese Master has put it, "When he opens his mouth, he is lost. When he seals his mouth, he is lost. If he does not open it, if he does not seal it, he is 108,000 miles from Truth." So long as there is a seeker, interpreting, evaluating, conceptualizing, he is thereby immediately in error and very far from Truth.

It is not so very difficult to understand, at least intellectually, that this universe is a dream. But it is almost impossible to accept that the one who is supposed to understand this is *himself a part of that dream*. This belief in oneself is the only real obstruction to the happening of the apperception, which comports the negation of the negator of the universe! Apperception means the sudden elimination of the bondage imposed by the "me"-concept. Ramana Maharshi has put it in his own inimitable way: "If in the process of awakening from sleep, you can hold your `identity', you shall indeed be awake, and forever." The elimination of the "me"-concept has also been strikingly put another way: "at the point of sleep when sleep has not yet come and external wakefulness vanishes, at this point *being* is revealed."

Ashtavakra continues along the same lines repeating his basic teaching over and over again, that Truth is always here-

and-now, transcending time and duration, and therefore, it is not something to be attained *by any* "one":

> *"No sooner does the person of dull intellect give up his practices of discipline and mind control, than he is assailed once again by the repressed desires and concepts."* (251)

> *"Even after listening to the Truth, the man of dull intellect does not give up his delusion. Through suppression, he may appear to be tranquil but his mind continues to be disturbed by cravings for sense-objects."* (252)

> *"He whose sense of personal doership has dropped off f through intuitive in-seeing of his nature, finds no reason to speak or do anything, even though in the eyes of the ordinary people he leads a normal working life."* (253)

> *"For the wise one with steadiness, who is ever unperturbed and fearless, where is the question of darkness or light? Can there be any question of his losing anything? For him, no thing exists."* (254)

> *"For him who has no personal nature of his own, and therefore whose nature cannot be described in specific terms, for such a Self-realized being, how can there be a question of patience, or discrimination, or even fearlessness?"* (255)

> *"In the yogic vision, there is neither heaven nor hell, not even the condition of jeevan-mukti, liberation in life. Indeed, in yogic Consciousness, in nothingness, no thing exists."* (256)

*"The mind of the steady one does not hanker for any
gain, nor does it grieve at something not attained.
His serene mind always remains filled with nectar."*
(257)

There are innumerable stories and anecdotes about the
Buddha (like all famous and infamous personalities), and
it is impossible to know which are true and which are not.
But it really does not matter, so long as the essence of the
story is grasped. There is one story about the Buddha which
has always appealed to me.

Gautama gave up a kingdom and all the pleasures of
life. He went to the other extreme, and even gave up eating
and undertook hard disciplinary practices. He became
physically very weak and mentally extremely lethargic.
One morning, while wandering, he felt so weak that he sat
leaning against the trunk of a tree. As he sat there, almost
falling into a coma, a group of village girls was passing along
the way, singing a popular tune, the gist of which was that
if you leave the strings of a musical instrument too loose,
you will not get the right sound, but if you pull them too
tight, they will break. Gautama suddenly had the intuitive
understanding then that the way was neither attachment
nor renunciation.

This "way" has been described as the "middle way",
but it is a misleading term, as no doubt the Buddha himself
realized at once. There is in fact neither a "way" nor the
middle of anything. If for practical reasons, the word "way"
must be used, it could only be described as the "inner way"
or the "transcendence way." The fact of the matter is that
neither words, nor symbols, nor sounds can ever accurately
indicate the Subjective State. The mere attempt to express
it—and therefore to objectify it—is moving away from
What-Is. The inherent limitation of words and symbols
must be understood and firmly kept in mind (which is
not as easy as it may sound for the "seeker"). Words and

symbols must necessarily be used. But once their sense has been apprehended, the words and symbols must be instantly dropped like hot coals.

Ashtavakra says, "No sooner does the person of dull intellect give up his practices of discipline and mind control, than he is assailed once again by repressed desires and concepts." What the sage emphasizes here is that whether the person of dull intellect (because he misses the point altogether) engages himself in the pursuit of *bhoga* (sensual pleasures) or *yoga* (disciplinary practices) the existence of the "me" in both activities ensures the continuance of desire. As it says in the *Bhagavad Gita*, "When a man lacks discrimination (a man of dull intellect, a *moodha*), his will wanders in all directions, in innumerable aims. Those who lack discrimination may quote the letter of the scripture, but they are really denying its inner truth. They are full of worldly desires and hungry for the rewards of heaven. They use beautiful figures of speech; they teach elaborate rituals which are supposed to obtain pleasure and power for those who practice them. But actually they understand nothing except the law of *karma* that brings about further births." Deliberate practices of discipline and control merely suppress desires and concepts, because there is a "me" conscious of doing these practices. The desires and concepts will always erupt with renewed vigor as soon as the practices are stopped.

It is only through understanding with great conviction that the individual separate entity is total illusion that desire and distractions are eliminated. It is what Milton has beautifully named "the sober certainty of waking bliss." Meister Eckhart put it thus: "A man must become truly poor and as free from his own creaturely will as he was when he was born. And I tell you, by the eternal truth, that so long as you *desire* to fulfil the will of God and have any hankering after eternity and God, for just so long you are not truly poor. He alone has true spiritual poverty who wills nothing, knows nothing, desires nothing." What does this mean? What exactly is one expected to do? The answer is, in the words of a seventeenth-century Frenchman *de Caussade*, "Do what you are doing now, suffer what you are suffering now; to do all this with holiness, nothing need be changed but your heart. Sanctity consists in *willing* what happens to us by God's order." In other words, you need do nothing. In fact, "you" must not "do" anything. Just accept—merely witness without judging—whatever is happening. Such acceptance will make you see the truth of the saying that when you begin to seek the *guru*, the *guru* has already been waiting for you. You will understand that the seeking is not of your choice but that the seeking itself is an impersonal event in the impersonal process of spiritual evolution, in which "you" are merely an instrument.

To repeat once again: whenever necessary, efforts will happen spontaneously. Efforts, when they are those of a "me" with a desire, must necessarily be fruitless.

In the words of Yoka Daishi:

"The philosophers indeed are clever enough, but wanting
in wisdom (moodha);
As to the others, they are either ignorant or puerile! They
take an empty fist as containing something real and
the pointing finger as the object pointed at.
Because the finger is adhered to as though it were the
Moon, all their efforts are lost."

The ultimate teaching will not be understood until you have it and then "you" will not want it.

A Muslim *fakir* has written a poem concerning Al-Hallaj Mansoor, a Sufi saint who was tortured and killed because he had declared, "I am God." The poem refers to a dream dreamt by someone who had participated in the killing of the saint. He saw that Al-Hallaj was being ceremoniously taken to heaven, and he could not understand it.

The poem reads:

O God! Why was a pharaoh condemned to the flames
for crying out "I am God"
and Hallaj is swept away to heaven
for crying out the same words: "I am God."
Then he heard a voice speaking:
When pharaoh spoke those words
he thought only of himself,
he had forgotten Me.
When Hallaj uttered those words—the same words -
he had forgotten himself.
He thought only of Me.
Therefore the "I am" in pharaoh's mouth
was a curse to him
and in Hallaj's the "I am"
is the effect of My grace.

Ashtavakra proceeds further on the matter of doing and personal effort. He says, even after listening to the Truth, the man of dull intellect does not give up his delusion (of a separate entity and personal effort). Through suppression, he may appear to be tranquil, but his mind continues to be disturbed by cravings for senseobjects. On the other hand, he whose essence of personal doership has dropped off through intuitive in-seeing of his real nature, finds no reason to speak or do anything, even though in the eyes of the ordinary people, he leads a normal working life. The Buddha walked thousands of miles and spoke thousands of words, but he neither walked one step nor uttered a single word. The meaningful phrase is "whose sense of personal doership has *dropped off* through intuitive in-seeing." No personal effort can make the sense of personal doership drop off.

The basic cause of all psychological misery is the basic separation between "Self" and "not-self", between "me" and "not-me", between "mine" and "not-mine." We are so conditioned to accept separation and boundaries as a natural phenomenon, that it is quite a surprise to suddenly be shown the world as it truly is. The world consists of only masses of land and masses of water. There are no visible lines of latitude and longitude. Nor can we see various colors demarcating the boundaries of the many nations! So, when the mystic—and today even the physicist—says that there is a basic oneness in the universe, he does not deny the magnificent variety in the phenomenal manifestation. What he does assert is that all objects in the cosmos are simply manifestations, in infinite variety, of the same oneness, be it called God, *Brahman*, Tao, Energy, or just Consciousness. Ashtavakra points out repeatedly that to see the universe as it is, any effort by the human being, (itself one kind of object in a variety of objects in the totality of the manifestation), must necessarily be futile, an exercise in frustration. It would be, as the Taoist says, like trying to wash off blood with blood. This understanding, whereby the problem is not solved but dissolved, can only happen, at the appropriate time, at the appropriate place, in an appropriate body-mind organism duly evolved to be able to receive this understanding. It can happen only through what might be called Grace. And once this understanding happens, all separation drops off, and the resulting state *phenomenally* is called by various names such as awakening, enlightenment, *nirvana*, *moksha* etc.

The ordinary person's vision of the spiritual plane beyond reality, as he knows and understands it, extends only to the dual concepts of heaven and hell. For the "higher" or more sophisticated seeker, his search extends beyond these interconnected opposites of heaven and hell into another concept of enlightenment, *jeevan-mukti*, liberation in phenomenal life. Ashtavakra goes beyond the concept of liberation or enlightenment. He says, in the yogic vision there is not only the absence of the interconnected opposites of heaven and hell, but even the absence of *jeevan-mukti*. The yogic vision is realization of the void as the ultimate absolute presence, which is the absence of the absence of both presence and absence.

Enlightenment cannot exist as an objective state for the simple reason that it is precisely what we all are: Consciousness. The Buddha has clearly stated that he had *attained* nothing whatsoever for the simple reason that there is nothing—no thing—to be attained. As phenomenal objects we could never "know" enlightenment. Nor can we "become" enlightenment. We cannot know it because knowing would be objective understanding (a phenomenal event) and we cannot become it because we *are* it. The core of the matter is that all seeking is done by a pseudo-subject seeking some thing. Yet neither the seeker nor that which he is seeking exists. In other words, even the concept of the void or emptiness disappears when conceptualization ceases altogether in the silence of the apperception (not perception, not comprehension) that all there is, is Consciousness.

Ashtavakra continues:

"The impartial one has neither praise for one who is considered good nor condemnation for one who is considered wicked. Contented and evenly balanced in happiness and misery, there is nothing for him to achieve." (258)

"The wise one neither abhors samsara *nor does he wish for* nirvana. *Free from the duality of joy and sorrow he is not concerned with birth or death."* (259)

"Glorious is the life of the wise one, free from all expectations, free from any attachment to wife, children or any other. He is free of all craving for sensual pleasure, who is unconcerned whether the body exists or not." (260)

"Contentment ever dwells in the heart of the steadfast one who is happy with whatever falls to his lot in life, who goes wherever life takes him, unmindful of where he happens to be at the end of the day." (261)

"Reposing on the foundation of his own true beingness, and therefore transcending birth and death, the great one does not care whether his body drops down dead or continues to exist." (262)

"Blessed is the wise one who stands aloof, who is attached to nothing, who is without any need for possessions, who has transcended the pairs of opposites, and all of whose doubts have been totally destroyed." (263)

Ashtavakra repeatedly lays great emphasis on the importance of desirelessness or detachment. Yet, at the same time that he describes it as the core of the wise man's behavior or attitude, he does not specifically ask the seeker to cultivate it. He is fully aware that desirelessness is not the direct cause of enlightenment but that enlightenment or the Self-awareness brings about desirelessness. Far be it for the sage to confuse cause and effect as does the ordinary person, the *moodha* (incidentally, it must be made clear at once that the *moodha* is not one by choice!). Desirelessness is certainly a condition precedent to the happening of the event called enlightenment, but the happening of such a condition is itself a matter of Grace.

In regard to Grace, Aldous Huxley has something very pertinent to say:

> "The help received by those who devotedly adore or pray to some personal saint, deity or Avatar is often not a genuinely spiritual grace, but a human grace" (I might add that even this "human grace" is part of the spontaneous process of spiritual evolution), "coming back to the worshipper from the vortex of psychic power set up by repeated acts of faith, yearning and imagination."

> "Spiritual Grace cannot be received continuously or in its fullness, except by those who have willed away their self-will" (even this must necessarily be a part of the impersonal process of spiritual evolution inasmuch as a body-mind organism simply cannot be expected to have any will or volition) "to the point of being able to truthfully to say 'not I, but God in me.' Spiritual grace originates from the divine Ground of all being, and *it is given* for the purpose of helping man to get to the end of the evolution, which is to return out of time into intemporality and recede from selfhood back to the impersonality of the divine Ground."

Enlightenment is not an object for an individual to achieve for his own. Here is a very beautiful passage from Chuang Tzu:

> Shun asked Cheng, saying, "Can one get Tao so as to have it for oneself?"

> "Your very body," replied Cheng, "is not your own. How should Tao be?"

> "If my body,'" said Shun, "is not my own, pray

whose is it?"

"It is the delegated image of God." replied Cheng, "Your life is not your own. It is the delegated harmony of God. Your individuality is not your own. It is the delegated adaptability of God. Your posterity is not your own. It is the delegated exuviae of God. You move, but know not how. You are at rest, but know not why. You taste, but know not the cause. These are the operations of God's laws. How then should you get Tao so as to have it for your own?"

In similar vein, here is what Lao Tzu, Chuang Tzu's Master has to say:

Push far enough towards the Void,

Hold fast enough to Quietness, And of the ten thousand things None but can be worked on by you.

I have beheld them, whither they go back. See, all things howsoever they flourish Return to the root from which they grew. This return to the Root is called Quietness; Quietness is called submission to Fate;

What has submitted to Fate becomes part of the always-so; To know the always-so is to be illumined; Not to know it means to go blindly to disaster.

That is what the Taoist Master Lao Tzu and his disciple Chuang Tzu have said from the non-dualist point of view of oneness.

Here is what Rabia, the Sufi woman-saint feels in terms of devotional theism:

God, if I worship Thee in fear o f hell, burn me in hell. And if I worship Thee in hope of Paradise, exclude me

from Paradise;
But if I worship Thee for Thine own sake, withhold not
Thine everlasting Beauty.

All three insist on the need for non-attachment to self-interest, the need for "holy indifference" (to use the corresponding Christian term), the need for a cheerful acceptance of affliction without either self-pity or wanting to return evil for evil. Ashtavakra describes the "steadfast one": Contentment ever dwells in his heart, he is happy with whatever falls to his lot in life, he who goes wherever life takes him "like a dry leaf in the breeze."

Whatever happens in the world is not judged on any pre-conceived standards of right and wrong (or any other opposites) by the awakened being. All that happens is merely witnessed as the functioning of Totality, in which the various individuals are merely instruments conceived and created with certain given inherent characteristics. Actions, therefore, are not seen by him as the actions of any particular individual. The wise man, the man of understanding, thus considers it irrelevant and unnecessary either to praise anyone or to condemn anyone since their actions are seen as *having just happened.* Having clearly apperceived the oneness of samsara and *nirvana,* it is immaterial for him whether the *samsara* exists or does not exist, or even whether his own body exists or does not exist. His basic understanding—which is also the ultimate understanding—comports the realization that all opposites are interrelated as a concept, and that their superimposition results not in a third thing but in a void. Thus the wise man does not think in terms of opposites like joy and sorrow, or birth and death, but accepts all events in the natural order of things.

In one beautiful verse, Ashtavakra has given an

exceedingly concise picture of the "enlightened person" in ordinary living:

> *"Blessed is the wise one who stands aloof (as the witnessing), who is attached to nothing, who is without any need for possessions, who has transcended the pairs of opposites, and all of whose doubts have been totally destroyed."*

Ashtavakra now comes to the concluding verses of this chapter. He says:

> *"Glorious is the one who is devoid of the feeling of me-and-mine, to whom a clod of earth, a precious stone and a bar of gold are all alike, the knots of whose heart have been rent asunder, and who has been purged of rajas and tamas." (264)*

The previous verse said, "whose doubts have been totally destroyed." In this verse, the sage uses the words "the knots of whose heart have been rent asunder." There is a verse in the *Mundakopanishad* (11-11-8) which says, "When he has seen both the higher and the lower (when his perception has gone beyond mere phenomenality), the knots of his heart become untied, all doubts are rent asunder and all his *karmas* have been destroyed." In the classical Hindu tradition, the human personality has been analytically considered as being bound by three powerful chords—*hridaya-granti* or knots of the heart—and that the human personality is conditioned by three delusory factors. The three chords are: "ignorance (*avidya*)" which breeds in the human psyche an inherent sense of inadequacy or imperfection, which is converted by the intellect into "desire (*kama*)", causing agitations in the mind which result in "physical activity (*karma*)." These three chords-ignorance, desire and personal activity—together constitute the bondage of misery (the concept of bondage) from which the human being further desires liberation!

According to the same tradition everything in the internal and external nature is governed by three attributes named *sattva, rajas* and *tamas*. The original nature is represented by sattva. The solution of continuity between the unmanifest and the manifest is obstructed by *rajas*, (volition, motivation, desire and activity) and by *tamas*, (inertia and ignorance). Unless, therefore, the covering (*avarana* and *vikshepa*) of *rajas* and *tamas*, that prevents the pure shining of *sattva*, is removed by the Grace of direct perception, true apperception cannot take place.

> "How can there be any comparison with the liberated one, in whose heart there are absolutely no remnants of desire of any kind, who is quite contented and totally indifferent towards all objects?" (265)

> "Can there be anyone else other than the one totally bereft of any personal desire, who knows and yet does not know, who perceives and yet does not perceive, who speaks and yet does not speak?" (266)

> "Be he a beggar or a king, glorious is he who is totally unattached and completely free from the conceptual duality of the interconnected opposites of good and evil." (267)

> "For the yogi who has realized his original nature and is therefore the embodiment of guileless sincerity, where is the question of licentiousness or restraint; where is the question of any determination of what is truth or what is not?" (268)

> "The inner experience of one who is totally desireless, who transcends all sorrow and continually abides

in the Self—how can it be described, and to whom
can it be described?" (269)

"The Self-realized one is not sleeping even when
he is asleep; he is not lying down even when he is
dreaming; he is not awake even in the waking state.
That is the state of the one who is contented in all
conditions." (270)

In answer to a question whether it was a fact that the
one who has realized his Self will not have the three states
of wakefulness, dream and deep sleep, Ramana Maharshi
made it clear that the three states will, and must during life
time, continue to exist for the body-mind organism. But the
Self-realized one is not identified with the body, and in all
the three states, he remains as the Self.

If you remain as you are now, you are in the wakeful
state. This is hidden in the dream state. The dream state
disappears when you are in deep sleep. The three states come
and go, but you are always there.

The Maharshi further explained that actually there
is only one state, that of Consciousness or awareness or
existence. The three states of waking, dream and deep
sleep are transient, but the real state continues to exist all
the time. What is present throughout is the impersonal
sense of presence. What is absent in the deep sleep state is
the personal sense of presence. Ramana Maharshi further
explained the point like this:

"Existence or Consciousness is the only reality.
Consciousness plus waking, we call waking.
Consciousness plus sleep, we call sleep. Consciousness
plus dream, we call dream. Consciousness is the
screen on which all pictures come and go. The screen
is real, the pictures are mere shadows on it...Because

the waking state is long, we imagine that it is our real state, but as a matter of fact, our real state is *turiya* or the fourth state which is always as it is and knows nothing of the three states of waking, dream or sleep. Because we call these *avasthas* (states), we call the fourth state also turiya avastha. But it is not an *avastha*, but the real and natural state of the Self. When this is realized, we know it is not a *turiya* or fourth state (a fourth state is only relative), but it is *turiyateeta*, the transcendent state."

—

"The man-of-wisdom is devoid of thought even when 11e is thinking; he is devoid of sense organs even when he is using them; he is devoid of intellect even though he is endowed with it. He is devoid of the ego, even though he possesses it." (271)

This verse points to the fact that even after enlightenment the body-mind organism through which enlightenment has happened continues to function as a phenomenal organism. For this organism to function, there must necessarily be an operational center whose function is to organize and direct the operations of the phenomenon of which it is in charge. Furthermore, for this organism to function in relation to other such human organisms, there must necessarily be an identity with each separate organism. Thus even the enlightened "person" must have such identity with a particular organism, for which form there is a name. In other words, even after enlightenment, the body-mind apparatus continues to "live" and responds to a particular name, and to that extent even the enlightened being identifies himself or herself to a particular body. To this extent the enlightened person thinks and acts and his sense organs function, precisely like any ordinary person. But there is a big difference which is not easily seen by the people among whom he lives. The ordinary person considers all thoughts as "his" thoughts, all actions as "his" actions, because he is identified with the body as a "me" and becomes attached to the various *affective* impulses arising in that psychic complex. He becomes identified with the operational center as a *separate entity*. This identification as a personal entity, as a separate doer with volition, is the cause of misery and the bondage. The man-of-wisdom, on the other hand, recognizes the separate operational center (generally considered to be in the "head") to be as phenomenal as the psycho-somatic organism itself, and therefore does not identify himself as a separate entity. For him, the event of enlightenment has revealed his real nature as the subjectivity which functions through the phenomenal center. All the functions that take place through the body are merely witnessed not as his personal actions but as part of the functioning of Totality.

This is what Ashtavakra means when he says that the man-of-wisdom is devoid of thought even when he is thinking (because he does not regard the thinking that takes place spontaneously as "his" thought); he is devoid of sense organs even when he is using them (because the sense organs belong to the body and their use is directed in the organism spontaneously by the phenomenal operational center and the man-of-wisdom is not "himself" using them); he is devoid of intellect even though he is endowed with it (because there is no personal desire or motivation of the man-of-wisdom behind the use of the intellect); he is devoid of the ego, even though he possesses it (because the ego extends only to the phenomenal operational center which is as phenomenal as the appearance itself, and not as a separate entity with a sense of personal doership).

"The man-of-wisdom is neither happy nor miserable,
neither attached nor unattached, neither liberated

nor an aspirant for liberation. He is neither this nor that." (272)

In this verse, all the sage points out is that the man-ofwisdom no longer exists as an individual entity for whom the opposites exist conceptually. The man-of-wisdom has transcended opposites, and therefore, he is "neither this nor that." In other words, the man-of-wisdom simply does not exist as a separate individual in phenomenality. This is elaborated further in the next verse.

"The blessed one is not distracted even in distraction; he is not meditative even in meditation; he is not dull even in a state of dullness; and he is not learned even though possessed of learning." (273)

"The liberated one who abides in the Self under all conditions, who is free of the concepts of action and duty, who is totally without desires, remains unconcerned with all actions that take place, and does not brood over what has been done and what has not been done." (274)

"When praised, the wise one does not feel pleased; when blamed, he is not angered. He neither rejoices in life nor does he fear death." (275)

"The serene one does not particularly seek either the crowds or the wilderness. He is the same anywhere in any conditions." (276)

CHAPTER TEN

※

Ashtavakra has completed his task of pointing to the Truth. He has obviously enjoyed this task because he had in the very beginning recognized the fact that King Janaka had reached the peak of evolution, and was ready for the final leap into the unknown. This dialogue between the Master and the highly evolved disciple illustrates very clearly the three principles of the relationship between the *guru* and the disciple: *shravana* (listening earnestly); *manana* (meditating on what is listened to, and getting the *genuine* doubts—not arguments for the sake of merely arguing— cleared up at least at the intellectual level, with sincerity, receptivity and humility); and finally, *nididhyasana* (letting the understanding settle down from the intellectual level into the deeper, intuitive level by not conceptualizing newer and fresher doubts). The process, therefore, begins with listening to the *guru*'s words with humility and an open, receptive mind—what Krishnamurti calls listening with a total mind—so that the listening becomes an intelligent listening without the barriers and obstacles of mechanical thought. Listening becomes intelligent when listening goes beyond mere words into what is below the surface of the words. The word "intelligence" comes from *inter* and *legcre* which means "to reach between"; the meaning in the dictionary is "mental alertness." Therefore listening intelligently means reading between the lines with alertness, without letting thought or thinking (which is merely a mechanical process in the brain) or conceptualizing interfere with the clarity of the *guru's* words.

Listening to the *guru's* words without the interruption of thought or conceptualizing does not mean being brainwashed. All it means is hearing the *guru's* words with great awareness so that misunderstanding is reduced to a minimum. The listening has to be followed by a critical examination. This must be done with an open mind, a mind untainted by preconceived notions and it must be done with the courage to face the new or fresh situations which the *guru's* words might create. Old notions, concepts, beliefs and opinions must be reexamined. Of course such doubts as may arise after such an honest examination should, indeed, be raised and a clarification be obtained. The *guru* speaks from experience, but words do have certain inherent limitations, particularly when speaking about Consciousness (*Brahman*).

As Adi Shankara has put it:

"There is no class of substance to which the *Brahman* belongs, no common genus. It cannot therefore be denoted by words which, like 'being' in the ordinary sense, signify a category of things. Nor can it be denoted by quality, for it is without qualities; nor yet by activity, because it is without activity—it is 'at rest, without parts or activity' according to the Scriptures. Neither can it be denoted by relationship, for it is 'without a second' and is not the object of anything but its own self. Therefore it cannot be defined by word or idea; as the Scripture says, it is the One 'before whom words recoil'."

Therefore, a critical examination of the *guru's* words must not be hampered by a lack of understanding of this basic limitation. What is needed in the attempt to understand is humility and faith in the *guru's* words.

The third part in the relationship between the *guru* and the disciple, after all reasonable doubts have been ironed out, is for the experiencing of the teaching to *happen*. The first two parts of this relationship refer to what the disciple is expected to "do." The third one is merely a consequential happening. Any active doing by the seeker to hasten the process will actually be an obstacle since any such positive act can only mean the continued existence of the identified "me." This process of the deepening of intellectual understanding into intuitive apperception may take various lengths of time in relativity depending upon the maturity of the seeker. But the very core of the understanding is that it can only happen on its own and not via the sweet will of the illusory seeker. The disciple in this case, the King Janaka, was so primed in receptivity that the very first words of the *guru* brought about sudden awakening. He erupted into an ecstatic outburst which must have, relatively speaking, gladdened the heart of Ashtavakra. Such a keen response from Janaka encouraged the outpouring of one hundred verses from Ashtavakra. In the final acceptance with gratitude, King Janaka in this concluding session gives vent to his own expression of the state of enlightenment.

Janaka responds to the great teaching of Ashtavakra, and in this outburst if the modern man finds a certain amount of flamboyant exuberance, it will be understood in its sincerity only by someone who has had a similar experience. If the body-mind organism, in which the event has happened, happens to be of a more passive nature, the response would perhaps not be quite so articulate but more in the nature of a spontaneous flow of tears.

Janaka says:

"Using the pincers of the apperception of Truth, I have extracted, from the innermost recesses of my heart, the painful thorn of diverse opinions, concepts

and judgments." (277)

*"Where is dharma, where is kama, where is artha?
Where is conscience and discrimination? Where is
duality or even non-duality—for Me who abide in
my own glory?" (278)*

*"Where is the past, where is the future or even the
present? Where is space? Where even eternity?—for
Me who abide in my own glory?" (279)*

*"Where is the Self and where the non-Self. Where,
likewise, are good and evil? Where is anxiety or
non-anxiety?—for Me who abide in my own glory?"
(280)*

*"Where is dreaming, where is deep sleep, and the
waking state? And where is the fourth state? Where
even is fear for Me who abide in my own glory?"
(281)*

*"Where is distance, where is proximity? Where is
exterior, where is interior? Where is the gross, and
where is the subtle? —for Me who abide in my own
glory?" (282)*

*"Where is life or death, where are the worlds, and
where the worldly relations? Where is the laya and
where is samadhi for Me who abide in my own
glory?" (283)*

Laya means the lapse of the mind into sleep, which
traditionally is considered one of the four obstacles to

samadhi, the other three being *vikshepa* (distraction), *kashaya* (torpidity) and *rasavada* (indulging in *samadhi*).

"To talk about the three goals of life is needless,
to talk about yoga is purposeless, and even to talk
about wisdom is irrelevant, for Me who abide in
the Self." (284)

"Where are the elements, where is the body, where
are the organs, and where is the mind? Where indeed
is the void, or despair for Me who am without the
slightest taint by nature?" (285)

"Where are the scriptures, and the knowledge of
the Self? Where is the mind detached from the
sense objects, and where is contentment? Where is
desirelessness?—for Me who has transcended the
duality of opposites?" (286)

"Where is knowledge and where is ignorance? Where
is I, and where 'this is mine'? Where is bondage and
where is liberation? How can there be any attribute
to my Self-nature?" (287)

"Where is prarabdha-karma? Where is the question
of liberation whether in life or at death?—for Me,
the ever undifferentiated?" (288)

Prarabdha-karma is the action which takes place
through a body-mind organism which is the effect of a past
action in the process of causation. Such action continues
to take place, but the Self-realized person does not regard
it as "his" action and is therefore not concerned with the
action as proper or improper, nor is he concerned with the
consequences as being acceptable or not acceptable.

"Where is the doer or the enjoyer, where is cessation of thought or the rising of thought? Where is the question of true perceiving or faulty perceiving for Me who am ever impersonal?" (289)

"Where is the world and where is the seeker, where is the question of yoga as knowledge, who is in bondage or who is liberated—for Me who am non-dual by his very nature?" (290)

"Where is creation and where is destruction? What is the end, and what is the means? Where is the question of seeking or achieving for Me abiding in my non-dual nature?" (291)

"Where is the 'knower' and where the 'means-to-knowledge'? Where is 'object of knowledge' and where 'objective knowledge'? What is any thing, and what is no thing -for Me who am ever pure?" (292)

"How can there ever be distraction or concentration, knowledge or delusion, joy or sorrow, for Me who am ever without action?" (293)

"Where is the relative or the absolute, happiness or misery, for Me who am ever beyond any conceptualization?" (294)

"Where is maya, where is samsara, where is attachment or detachment, how can there be any question of jiva or Brahman —for Me who am ever pure?" (295)

"Where is activity or inactivity, where is liberation or bondage for Me who am ever immutable, indivisible and established in the Self?" (296)

"Where are spiritual instructions or scriptural injunctions? Where is the disciple and where is the guru? Where indeed is the question of any duty for Me, the subjective potential plenum, free from all limitations?" (297)

"Where is existence or non-existence? Where is unicity or duality? In short, it is needless to say anything more, other than that nothing indeed emanates from Me." (298)

In all these verses, the underlying central point in what Janaka says is that there has occurred a transcending over the duality of opposites.

One recollects the outpouring of gratitude from Saint Jnaneshwar to his older brother and *guru* Nivrittinatha:

This state has negated not only the duality of phenomenality and non-phenomenality but all other interrelated concepts and dualities of name and form.

The conceptual duality of Shiva and Shakti have negated each other and merged in this state.

All objects and all words have merged in this state and conceptualization has also ceased.

0, my Lord *guru*, what a state you have brought me into, in which I am the giver and I am the taker, I am both the giving and the taking.

The wonder of it all is that you have awakened one who was never asleep, and put one to sleep who was never awake.

You and I are not different, yet out of your love and affection you call me your own. Since I have no existence apart from you, this demonstration of duality within the Unicity is your unique achievement.

What Janaka says in fact is that a complete transformation has occurred in his case through listening to his *guru*. And more importantly, he says that this is an impersonal happening in which the *guru*, the disciple and the teaching itself, are all three purely phenomenal instruments. What this means is that in this *metanoesis*, this *para-vrittie*, the "180-degree-turnaround" is not *done* at all. It is certainly not done by any "you" as an entity, and therefore, it is an impersonal happening, a turning over from the duality of positive and negative into the void of *Unicity*.

What Janaka is saying is that since it is not he, as an individual, who is knowing, seeing, looking, doing, it makes no difference to him whether there is knowing or not knowing, seeing or not seeing, looking or not looking, doing or not doing. There is only witnessing of whatever is known, looked at, or done (positively or negatively), as part of the functioning of Totality. He is that Noumenal potential which becomes phenomenally present where there is a "vacant" mind, when there is no volitional doing or not-doing.

Indeed, what Janaka is pointing out (in his apperception of Truth as eloquently propounded by his *guru*, Ashtavakra) in grateful appreciation, is that basic fact that any object as such can never be either good or not good. The two dual attributes arise only in the cognizing of it *by the split-mind* in which there is a supposed cognizer and some thing cognized. Actually there is neither a subject-cognizer nor an object-cognized: all there is, is cognizing of which the two are dual aspects, and such cognizing is a Noumenal functioning.

What Janaka is doing in these verses, is listing the various interdependent counterparts, the various negative and positive concepts of opposites, and, superimposing the opposing elements of each concept, he produces a mutual annihilation. He talks about the various opposites, all of which represent aspects of the split-mind in the process of conceptualization (or creation of images in the mind) which may be termed dualism. By superimposing those opposites, Janaka arrives at their mutual annihilation. The result is the healing of the split-mind into its wholeness, which is called enlightenment. It is a return from the personal to the impersonal, from the individual to the universal.

Janaka's irrefutable conclusion is that the only ultimate understanding (which itself ultimately would be negated in the void of silence) is that nothing is. No thing or object whatsoever exists, not even himself as an individual object. This means that total phenomenal absence is itself total Noumenal presence. No more can or need be said, for ultimately all we can ever know is *neti-neti*—not this, not that.

An exceedingly neat and clear-cut summary of the Advaita teaching of non-duality comes from the Tao Master Hui, in answer to a relevant question:

"Perceiving the *Buddhakaya* means ceasing to perceive anything as existing or not existing... Existence is a term used in contradistinction to non-existence, while non-existence is used in opposition to existence. Unless one begins to accept the first concept as valid, the other cannot stand. Similarly, without the concept of nonexistence, how can that of existence have any meaning? These two owe their being to mutual dependence and pertain to the realm of birth and death. It is just by avoiding such dual perceiving that we may come to behold the real *Buddhakaya*."

As soon as we begin to use words as language, we are dealing not with a phenomenon but with a concept. It is only in deep silence that we leave concepts behind. In other *words(!!)*, as Janaka says in the very first verse, the words of the *guru* have been used merely as the instrument to rid the innermost recesses of the heart of the concepts, opinions (words). He means that once the *guru*'s words were used as an instrument, the instrument was thrown away. There was no need to keep repeating the words like a *mantra*, which would have meant an ineffective use of the *guru*'s words. As Ramana Maharshi often said, the *guru*'s words are to be used like a thorn to remove the thorn of concepts embedded in the heart, and thereafter both the thorns are to be thrown away That is why in every verse thereafter, he keeps repeating that once the embedded thorn of concepts was removed, he was abiding in the Self and was no longer concerned with any concept of the interrelated opposites. He has seen phenomenality as nothing but a great dream in which the individual is merely a character without any substantial existence. Once phenomenality is seen as the illusion that it is, it has been transcended and what remains is the void of absolute silence. In this silence, the very *mahavakya*, "I am the *Brahman*", becomes an irrelevance. With the transcendence of phenomenality itself, all dualities which form the basis of phenomenality necessarily lose all significance. Indeed, the mechanism of phenomenality—the concept of space-time—also becomes quite useless. It is relegated to the junk heap along with all other concepts.

www.Advaita.org

Lightning Source UK Ltd.
Milton Keynes UK
UKOW02f2337290816

281771UK00001B/33/P